C000196023

Critical Guides to French Texts

50 Voltaire: Lettres philosophiques

Critical Guides to French Texts

EDITED BY ROGER LITTLE, WOLFGANG VAN EMDEN, DAVID WILLIAM

VOLTAIRE

Lettres philosophiques

Dennis Fletcher

Professor of French,
University of Durham

Grant & Cutler Ltd
1986

I.S.B.N. 84-599-1110-1

DEPÓSITO LEGAL: V. 2.030 - 1985

Printed in Spain by
Artes Gráficas Soler, S.A., Valencia
for
GRANT & CUTLER LTD
11 BUCKINGHAM STREET, LONDON W.C.2

Contents

Contents

Prefatory Note

All references to the *Lettres philosophiques* are to René Pomeau's easily accessible edition (Paris, Garnier-Flammarion, No. 15, 1964). Those which refer to Letters I-XXIV indicate number of letter and page: V, p.42. References to the twenty-fifth letter (the 'remarques' on Pascal's *Pensées*) indicate the remark and the page number: RXXVI, p.174. Italicised numbers in brackets refer to the items in the Select Bibliography. References in the form D123 are to letters in Theodore Besterman's definitive edition of Voltaire's correspondence (*Complete Works of Voltaire*, Voltaire Foundation, vols 85-135, 1968-1977). The spelling in quotations from these letters has been modernised.

1 Text and Context

Relating text to context is essential for a proper understanding of the *Lettres philosophiques*. The work originated in Voltaire's experience of England, which is its principal though not exclusive frame of reference. This English context quickly makes its presence felt to any editor faced with the task of choosing a basic text from among those of the earliest editions of the work. Three of these editions need to be mentioned: the *Letters Concerning the English Nation*, published in London in 1733; *Lettres écrites de Londres sur les Anglais et autres sujets*, supposedly published in Basle but actually in London in 1734; and the *Lettres philosophiques*, published in 1734 by Jore in Rouen under a false imprint (Lucas, Amsterdam). The Jore edition is the only one of these to include the 'anti-Pascal' as Voltaire called his reflections on Pascal's *Pensées* which make up the twenty-fifth of the *Lettres philosophiques*. These remarks on Pascal would certainly have been included in the Basle (London) edition and justified the reference to 'autres sujets' in its title, if Voltaire had entrusted the arrangements for its publication to someone more energetic and reliable than his friend Thieriot, who had the task of seeing both French and English versions of Voltaire's work through the press. This was one of the reasons why Gustave Lanson chose the Jore text as the basis for his excellent and still unsurpassed critical edition of 1909 and why it has been chosen (in R. Pomeau's Garnier-Flammarion edition) for this critical guide.

It has been suggested by A.-M. Rousseau (*27*, p.46) that the first two of the editions mentioned above deserve to oust the Jore text from its privileged position and to form the basis of a bi-lingual edition with French and English texts on facing pages. This idea is given added weight by the acceptance on the part of most Voltaire scholars of Harcourt Brown's thesis (*9*) that the *Letters Concerning the English Nation*, so long regarded as a translation by an English hand of the French edition published in London under Thieriot's supervision, are, in fact, for the most part Voltaire's own original work. (The reader of Voltaire's correspondence now has to keep on the alert in order to decide whether a reference to his 'lettres anglaises' or 'lettres sur les Anglais' applies to the original English version of the Letters or to the French text based on it.) Lanson's choice, however, remains firmly grounded: the Jore edition retains its superiority as an *œuvre de combat*, a faithful mirror of Voltaire's intentions. These are indeed *Lettres philosophiques* which more truly reflect the mind of the emergent *philosophe* than those '*Lettres anglaises* — et parfois *philosophiques*', as A.-M. Rousseau describes them, which nevertheless need to be rehabilitated and set beside the Lanson edition.

The origins of the *Lettres philosophiques* go back to Voltaire's stay in England from May 1726 to November 1728. He returned to France with a substantial body of material for publication. This material included a certain number of first drafts of some of the *Lettres*. These were left in the background for a time while he was busy with other works and it was not until 1732 that he began the final stages of composition. By December of that year, it becomes clear from his correspondence that he had decided upon the three-pronged publishing offensive on the European commercial market which was to produce in 1734 the Basle (London) and Amsterdam (Rouen) editions, and the *Letters Concerning the English Nation* which preceded them in 1733.

The circumstances which led to Voltaire's stay in this country need to be recalled briefly since they have some bearing upon his attitude to his new environment and the impact which it made upon him. In 1725, at 31, the bourgeois François Arouet had every reason for feeling on top of the world. With his *Oedipe* (1718) and *La Ligue* (1723 — generally known from 1724 as *La Henriade*) he had scaled the twin peaks of tragedy and epic poetry, the two 'noble' genres in the literary hierarchy, and had become accustomed to rubbing shoulders with the great in the heady atmosphere of the Court. His mode of life seemed to justify the noble appendage 'de Voltaire' which he had adopted some years before. A tart retort to the gibe of status-seeker thrown at him by a true-born noble, the chevalier de Rohan, however, led to a beating administered by the chevalier's lackeys which left him with his pride hurt more than his person. His frantic desire for revenge produced an unfavourable reaction from his supposed friends among the aristocracy. Luckily, he still had some real friends in high places upon whom he could rely. After allowing him to suffer the relatively mild unpleasantness of incarceration in the Bastille for twelve days, they complied with his request for permission to embark for England. Hérault, the *lieutenant général de police*, a former schoolmate of Voltaire's at the Collège Louis-le Grand demonstrated the efficacy of the old boy network by making the whole operation look like an officially enforced exile.

Why did Voltaire choose to go to England? In the first place, this decision is quite understandable if one considers the gruesome alternative of some provincial backwater. Constrained to remain at least fifty leagues away from Paris, he could still avoid such social and cultural deprivation. In much of his later life his activities would serve to keep him in the mainstream of French cultural life but also to debar him from residence in Paris, to say nothing of appearing at Court, though he never gave up either of these ideas. The most acceptable substitute for the sort of existence which had suddenly been denied him in France in 1726 was clearly available to him across the Channel.

The ambivalence in Voltaire's attitude to the question of his social station meant that he could at one and the same time resent the caste-bound society of eighteenth-century France and aspire to a less precarious place in its hierarchy. The *gens d'épée* of his own nation looked down upon him as a mere scribbler, one of the *gens de plume*. This led him to speculate about the mentality of members of high society in other countries and the degree of their acceptance of writers like himself. His curiosity had already been aroused by visits to Holland in 1713 and 1722, which gave him his first taste of a comparatively free society. It was increased, towards the end of 1722, by his first meeting with a highly cultured representative of the English aristocracy, whose charisma ensured a deep and lasting influence upon the young poet.

The initial impact of Henry St John, Viscount Bolingbroke, upon Voltaire was nothing short of electrifying to judge by the latter's excited report of the encounter (D135). From this meeting at La Source, the country house near Orléans of the exiled elder statesman, one can trace the subsequent philosophical apprenticeship of Voltaire based upon an instant hero worship of his mentor, 'un des plus brillants génies et l'homme le plus éloquent de son siècle', as he was to describe him later. The influence of Bolingbroke is discernible in the *Lettres philosophiques* not only in direct references but also, in a more pervasive form, in the work's fundamental character and its significance in relation to the evolution of Voltaire as a writer. Bolingbroke can be seen in the years 1723-24 striving to give Voltaire's interests a more philosophical orientation. In a letter of June 1724 (D190) he encourages the poet to apply himself to the study of Locke's *Essay on Human Understanding* and directs his attention away from Descartes and Malebranche, who are characterised as 'plutôt poètes que philosophes', towards Newton.

The cosmopolitan literary taste of the English *milord* is admired by the visitor to La Source in terms (D135) which will be echoed in the final paragraph of the twenty-second *lettre philosophique*. The fact that the host also responded enthusiastically to Voltaire's readings from the *Henriade* on that occasion clearly helped to establish a good relationship. Bolingbroke's enthusiasm encouraged his friend to publish the poem surreptitiously, and his support would certainly have enhanced in Voltaire's eyes the appeal of England as a venue for a more impressive publication by subscription along the lines of the successful enterprise of his great rival, the poet Jean-Baptiste Rousseau, during a six month visit in 1723. Such a venture would have appeared eminently credible in the light of Bolingbroke's influence and contacts. Furthermore, the friendship with Bolingbroke could not fail to have opened up for him the enticing prospect of an assured entrée to the circle of his English friends, which included the major figures of Pope and Swift.

Let down by bankrupt financiers, Voltaire was to experience a dispiriting introduction to England. 'I was without a penny, sick to death of a violent ague, a stranger, alone, helpless, in the midst of a city wherein, I was known to nobody. My lord and my lady Bolingbroke were in the country...I had never undergone such distress', he recalled later (D303). Voltaire's deep depression in the spring of 1726 is manifest in the obsessive interest in the English penchant for suicide which pervades his correspondence and finds an echo in the translation of Hamlet's famous soliloquy in the eighteenth *lettre philosophique*. By the summer of 1726, however, that irrepressible 'curiosité d'un homme raisonnable' referred to in the opening sentence of the *Lettres philosophiques* had generated a lively appreciation of a country where men can think freely. 'Si je suivais mon inclination, ce serait là que je me fixerais dans l'idée seulement d'apprendre à penser' (D299), he confesses.

Permanent residence in England, one feels, was not just a passing fancy on Voltaire's part. The objective of learning the language was pursued all the more vigorously by him since he believed that 'apprendre à penser' implied 'apprendre à penser en anglais'. A considerable degree of success, if we are to believe him, crowned these efforts. In the dedication (to Bolingbroke) of his play *Brutus* (1731) he testifies: 'J'avais passé près de deux ans dans une étude continuelle de votre langue...Je m'étais presque accoutumé à penser en anglais'. This testimony, backed up not only by his *Essay on Epick Poetry* and his *Essay upon Civil Wars in France* but also by the considerable volume of his correspondence in English, tends to be supported by the admittedly somewhat over-generous judgement of Chetwood, the prompter at Drury Lane, on Voltaire's progress: 'In four or five months he not only conversed in elegant English but wrote it with exact propriety'. *Pace* Dr Norma Perry, whose researches (*19, 20, 21*) into Voltaire's extensive contacts with his exiled compatriots in England remain invaluable, it seems more than plausible that the author of the *Letters Concerning the English Nation* had prepared himself for the task of composition by thorough immersion in the English cultural atmosphere.

The idea of 'going native' squares with that of flattering the

English readers of his *Letters*, in the preface to which we read: 'The high esteem which Mr de Voltaire has always discover'd for the English is a Proof how ambitious he is of their Approbation'. The business acumen of Voltaire, apparent in the promotional aspect of the two *Essays* designed to stimulate subscription for the *Henriade* in 1728, should not blind us however to his genuine admiration for the English way of life. The picture of England which we have in the *Lettres philosophiques* is inspired by the conviction that things were on the whole ordered better there than in France. Voltaire's compatriots are being invited to learn from England's example. The accuracy of Voltaire's picture is open to question from the outset. His patriotism (never of the 'my country, right or wrong' variety) finds expression in criticisms, both implicit and overt, of his native land which often appears benighted in comparison with its neighbour. The roseate view of life produced by the security and comfort of the gracious country-house of a wealthy silk merchant of Wandsworth, Everard Fawkener, colours the *Lettres philosophiques*, the first drafts of which were written there. The piquant ingredient of English eccentricity which bulks large in what is probably a discarded draft (see *1*, II, pp.256-65) is still present in the first four *lettres philosophiques*, but the crankiness of the Quakers is clearly mitigated by their shining virtues and not presented as a trait of the national character.

René Pomeau (*24*) has traced the evolution of Voltaire's conception of the *Lettres philosophiques* from his initial project in 1726 of delineating the character of 'this strange people', the English (D303), to the later one (described in the 1728 Advertisement preceding his two *Essays*) of concentrating upon 'the useful things and the extraordinary Persons' to be observed in England. The utilitarian standpoint will be dominant in the *Lettres* and among the 'extraordinary Persons' mentioned, Locke and Newton will receive lengthy homage while Tillotson, Milton and Boyle will sink without trace. Other unnamed statesmen and great commanders promised a place in Voltaire's survey (a promise repeated later in the twelfth *lettre philosophique*) will not appear either.

Having considered the option of the traveller's tale and that of the guide to foreigners replete with colourful descriptive detail, Voltaire rejects both in favour of crisp and incisive analysis of the collective mentality of the English and its reflections in their social, political and intellectual life. His didactic ardour, in harmony with his polemical intent, ensures that his presentation of England will be more a militant statement than an anodyne portrait. The subversive elements of those of his works which appeared before his stay in England — the *Henriade, Le pour et le contre, Oedipe* — already point towards the ritual burning by the public executioner in 1734 of those 'Lettres philosophiques, politiques, critiques, poétiques, hérétiques et diaboliques', as Voltaire described them (D1234), which were to become a major text in the history of the Enlightenment.

2 Voltaire's England

Broadly speaking, the 24 letters which Voltaire devotes to his presentation of England fall into four groups: Letters I-VII deal with religion, VIII-XI with government and society, XII-XVII with philosophy and science and XVIII-XXIV with literature and culture. This tidy division credits the author with rather more concern for thematic cohesion than is warranted by even a brief glance at the titles of the letters, but it will serve as a convenient framework for an analysis of his view of British civilisation.

(i) *Religion*

Voltaire's view of organised religion as a whole was jaundiced enough to inhibit a positive attraction to the form it might take in any particular country. England in this respect offered him the least of possible evils, not the best of possible worlds. 'C'est ici le pays des sectes. Un Anglais, comme homme libre, va au Ciel par le chemin qui lui plaît' (V, p.42). Freedom of worship here appears in a good light as part of the fabric of a free country's way of life. Important reservations follow, however. Sectarian strife was not unknown in England, witness the upheaval of the Civil War, and more recently, at the time of the Sacheverell trial (1710), the violent riots in which the mob looted Dissenting (Nonconformist) chapels in response to the inflammatory sermon for which this defender of exclusive privileges for the established Church had been impeached. Calm had descended upon the England to which Voltaire had been introduced in 1726, but he is aware, as this fifth letter shows, that what civil rights an Englishman enjoyed depended on the religious denomination to which he belonged. He could choose his own path to heaven, but if he was a Dissenter he was likely to live his life on earth as a second-class citizen, or if a Catholic as a third-class citizen.[1]

From Voltaire's vantage-point the prospect still seemed bright enough. The privileged constitutional position of the established Anglican Church and the monopoly of political power which enabled it to be tolerant of its impotent rivals appeared to him as an unmitigated good. In his basically sound analysis of the decline of Nonconformity, which he relates to the Quakers in particular (IV, p.40), the key factor is the young Quakers' natural desire to enjoy the material goods of this world. The same motivation explains the defection to the Church of England of Dissenters from other sects. These 'conversions' are welcomed by Voltaire the cynical realist who sees such unheroic lack of fanaticism as producing a quiet revolution in which all the conflicting sects are eventually assimilated by one dominant state-controlled religion.

Erastianism (the belief that the state should have authority over the Church in ecclesiastical matters) provides the thread of Voltaire's thought in the fifth and sixth paragraphs of Letter V. One may detect here a muted echo of a resounding debate which had taken place some years before Voltaire's visit: the Bangorian controversy, sparked off by the Erastian opinions of Benjamin Hoadly, Bishop of Bangor, a staunch supporter of the Whigs. Hoadly's political stance reflects the Latitudinarian Low Church outlook of the Upper House of Convocation (the governing body of the Anglican Church): a broadly tolerant and undogmatic attitude with the accent on the reasonable and practical aspects of Christian ethics. The censure of Hoadly's opponents in the Lower House of Convocation, a hot-bed of High Church Toryism, in 1717 brought about the suspension of the entire body until the middle of the nineteenth century. Voltaire's account is somewhat muddled: the Lower House of Convocation ('l'assemblée du bas clergé') is not distinguished from the Upper House, which is never mentioned. 'La Chambre Haute' to which he refers is the House of Lords, and the crucial political role of the bishops in this assembly is totally misconstrued. Voltaire does not appreciate the fact that 24 (out

---

[1]For a lucid account of discrimination against Nonconformists and disabilities imposed upon Roman Catholics at this time, see W.A. Speck (*33*, Chapter 4).

of a total of 26) regularly found themselves obliged to repay (by attendance at the House) the debt they owed to the Whig oligarchy for their preferment. Hoadly's views, Bolingbroke had noted, made a bishop merely a layman with a crook in his hand. Voltaire quotes (V, p.43) a similarly Erastian remark emanating from his noble friend and thus makes his own position clear, even if his account of the situation is not entirely so.

The ease with which the dominant Anglican Church accommodated a wide internal diversity of opinion on theological matters made it appear to Voltaire as a half-way house between the 'petit troupeau' of enlightened spirits (Letter VII), whose rejection of the doctrine of the Trinity brought them considerably nearer to his own 'natural religion', and the mass of zealots and bigots to be found in the ranks of the Presbyterians (Letter VI) and to a lesser extent among the Quakers (Letters I-IV). Voltaire's own religious views were diametrically opposed to the Presbyterians' gloomy Calvinistic doctrines which offered none but a select few of the faithful the divine and unfathomable grace which allowed escape from eternal torments. He particularly abhorred their grimly kill-joy attitude towards the use of leisure. His presentation of this sect is rendered even more unfavourable by the suggestion that their contempt for worldly goods and social advancement is hypocritical. Greed and avarice are well-nigh inseparable in Voltaire's mind from the clerical mentality; he takes it as entirely natural that an Anglican bishop should live in luxury if he could and that a Presbyterian minister who could not should rail against him out of sheer envy.

Broadly speaking, the religious situation in Hanoverian England provided plenty of scope for greed, avarice and envy. Voltaire's own low opinion of the mercenary priesthood of his own country is reflected in his caustic allusion to the Catholic 'ceremony' of collecting tithes which is diligently practised by the Anglican clergy (Letter V) and his implicit approval of the Quaker's somewhat indignant rejection (Letter II) of the idea of hiring intermediaries to carry out duties which he believes are the responsibility of each individual Christian. Quakers, in fact, were regularly sent to prison for following the dictates of their conscience and refusing to pay tithes. The ambitious and power-hungry ecclesiastic provides an obvious target for the anti-clerical Voltaire, yet his sketchy account of promotion prospects misleads as much by what it leaves out as by what it includes. Long service in the Church, the only means of advancement which he cites, was far less important than the political service which he entirely omits to mention. The unworldly pedant, devoid of social grace and ill at ease with the fair sex, makes a good foil for the womanising French *abbé* whose hectic sowing of wild oats leaves little time for spiritual concerns (V, p.44). The young Anglican climber with an eye upon a chaplaincy which would give the entrée to the world of politics and high society and allow him to rise quite quickly in the ecclesiastical hierarchy would have provided a closer match. The avarice which Voltaire associates with the higher dignitaries of the Church is not enlarged upon. The system of pluralism (and non-residence) which allowed ecclesiastics to accumulate preferments certainly facilitated the building up of a sizeable fortune, but he would seem to have had no knowledge of this practice.

If pluralism was a luxury for the occasional rapacious bishop, it was a vital necessity for the far more common figure of the impoverished country clergyman, who, faced with a situation where more than half the livings available were worth less than £50 a year, was forced to hold more than one to make ends meet. There is little evidence to suggest that Voltaire had any direct acquaintance with the lower orders of clergy. His references to them convey the idea that they are a rather torpid breed, whose mundane marital existence is occasionally marked by a solitary excursion to the ale-house to get decently drunk. Their lukewarm religious life is part of the general atmosphere of 'un âge où le monde est rassasié de disputes et de sectes' (VI, p.51). In an England where sleeping dogs are systematically allowed to lie, Convocation is also laid to rest and its burning of impious books relegated to the past. Voltaire evidently approves of a situation where a Protestant divine like Dr Samuel Clarke merely forfeits the chance of preferment to high ecclesiastical office by publishing his unorthodox opinions, without having to go to the stake for them — which was the fate reserved for such 'vilains hérétiques, à brûler à tous les diables' (V, p.44) in a less tolerant country.

In the dialogue which so enlivens the first letter, the old Quaker is quickly reminded by his conventionally pious and outraged interlocutor that his views on baptism would earn him death by burning 'en pays d'Inquisition'. The 'impious' exposition that follows establishes that this sect, which recognises the Scriptures as the sole source of authority for their religion and rejects all the sacraments as mere accretions attributable to commentators upon holy writ, has been chosen by Voltaire as the natural spearhead of his offensive against orthodox Christianity. The choice underlines the supreme importance he attached to his propagandist objective; the Quakers judged by any other criterion would merit neither the pride of place nor the amount of space which Voltaire has given them in this work. The bulk of the Dissenters in the early eighteenth century was made up of the 300,000 or so Baptists, Independents and Presbyterians; the 50,000 Quakers were one of the lesser denominations. Their claim upon the attention of Voltaire's compatriots may be justified by the singularity of their beliefs and behaviour, which made up another thread in the rich tapestry of eccentricity which the civilisation of this 'strange people' offered the foreign observer. This formed only part of their attraction for Voltaire. Far more important to him was their value chiefly as a model but also, in some respects, as a cautionary example. The Quaker inspired to stand up and utter gibberish arouses the curiosity of that 'homme raisonnable' to whom we are introduced in the opening sentence of the first letter, but he also offends his reason. The tolerance of the Quaker congregation mitigates the absurdity of this spectacle for him, just as the modesty and politeness of his Quaker guide make his over-zealously selective citing of Scripture a little more acceptable. Basically, however, the Quaker's contention 'qu'il n'y a point de christianisme sans une révélation immédiate' (II, p.27) is rejected. The mumbo-jumbo of 'divine' inspiration, shown up as a charade in the presentation of George Fox in Letter III, serves to put the Quakers into the same camp as the Presbyterians, whose nasal whining from the pulpit, absurd attachment to unimportant sartorial details and austere distaste for innocuous social pleasures serve to strengthen this affinity. The third letter with its picture of mass-hysteria, physical convulsions and so-called miracles may be related to the antics of the Jansenist 'convulsionnaires de Saint-Médard' abhorred by Voltaire as illustrating the same truth: 'l'enthousiasme est une maladie qui se gagne' (III, p.31).

So much on the debit side. It is evident, however, that Voltaire respects 'la vertu sous des apparences ridicules' (VI, p.36) and gives the Quakers due credit for their staunch pacificism, spirit of charity, tolerance and brotherly love, practical concern for man's essential duties, respect for the laws of the land and determination to get on in the world through the pursuit of trade and commerce. His ultimate ideal may well be mirrored in the idyllic, Arcadian society of Pennsylvania, which will be recalled by the utopian Eldorado of his *Candide*: 'un souverain que tout le monde tutoyait, et à qui on parlait le chapeau sur la tête, un gouvernement sans prêtres, un peuple sans armes, des citoyens tous égaux, à la magistrature près, et des voisins sans jalousie' (IV, p.38). As a political realist, however, he proposes a more accessible model to his fellow-countrymen, one which could be developed out of the existing Gallican church by following the guide-lines offered by England. In his *Examen important de milord Bolingbroke* (1767), the English oracle will be made to repeat what he had said in his *Philosophical works* (1754): 'on doit laisser subsister la hiérarchie établie par un acte de parlement, en la soumettant toujours à la législation civile, et en l'empêchant de nuire'. The Erastian echo of the fifth *lettre philosophique* could not be clearer.

(ii) *Government and Society*

In Letters VIII and IX Voltaire deals with the system of government in contemporary England. His visit coincided with a period of vigorous political controversy in the national press over the way in which limited monarchy should operate. The campaign of opposition to Walpole and the Whig oligarchy was led outside parliament from 1726 by Bolingbroke and Pulteney

in their journal *The Craftsman*, whilst Walpole's supporters
counter-attacked in *The London Journal* and elsewhere. The
conflicting interpretations of the British constitution offered by
each side revolved around the twin concepts of the mixed state,
partaking of the nature of monarchy, aristocracy and
democracy, and the balance which was supposed to result from
the interplay of the different components of this system of
government. Montesquieu, who visited England a few years
later than Voltaire, was to make his observation of British
political life and, more particularly, his reading of the polemical
journalism of the time the basis for his influential doctrine of the
separation of powers. Voltaire, no less aware of the topics of
political discussion, takes up these same concepts somewhat less
purposefully to support a view of free political institutions
resulting from a nation's centuries of struggle against absolute
government and its eventual success, with the Revolution of
1688, in establishing the only constitutional monarchy in the
world. This historical perspective is the thread which links the
two letters. The Civil War, briefly evoked by the reference to
Cromwell at the end of Letter VII, is at the centre of Voltaire's
commentary in Letter VIII upon the conflict between king and
parliament sparked off by the monarch's ill-advised attempt to
become master of the ship when he should have been content to
be merely its chief pilot. The rule of law founded upon the
Revolution settlement reflects the determination of the English
people to safeguard the freedom which they had won at the cost
of so much civil strife and bloodshed. The execution of Charles I
is presented at the end of Letter VIII as an example of
parliament as the resolute court of the nation sitting in
judgement upon a royal malefactor and dispassionately making
the punishment fit the heinous crime of resorting to arbitrary
rule. In Letter IX Voltaire traces the commons' long history of
subjection to tyrants, great and small, secular and clerical, and
their gradual acquisition of power which in the all-important
area of the nation's finances has made them the linchpin in the
constitutional machinery of the legislative process.

There is every reason to suppose that Voltaire was well-
acquainted with *The Craftsman* while he was in England. We

know from his correspondence that he continued to receive the journal after his return to France. It is not altogether a coincidence, perhaps, that in one of its first numbers *The Craftsman* introduced a parallelism between Roman and English history and that the first half of Voltaire's eighth *lettre philosophique* is composed around a comparison between ancient Rome and modern Britain. It is interesting that the alleged financial corruption of some members of parliament should be singled out by Voltaire as the only feature which justifies members of this body comparing themselves to ancient Romans, since this corruption was constantly being denounced by *The Craftsman* as a grave danger to the British constitution. Voltaire moves on without further probing, however, to his pet subject of religion. He contrasts the English Civil War, successful in bringing freedom to the nation but blighted by emanating from a religious source, with the Roman civil wars, devoid of religious motivation but producing only servitude. He then turns to an analysis of the British constitution set out in the familiar terms of a highly successful distribution of the powers of government between king, lords and commons. He describes 'cette balance': 'La Chambre des Pairs et celle des Communes sont les arbitres de la nation, le Roi est le sur-arbitre' (VIII, p.55). Voltaire could have read in Jonathan Swift's *A Discourse of the Contests and Dissentions between the Nobles and the Commons in Athens and Rome* (1701) about the superiority of mixed government. He does not follow its diagnosis of Rome's decline, however. Swift attributes the downfall of Rome to the upsetting of the balance of power through an increase of the influence of the *plebs* at the expense of the patricians and the consequent emergence of tyrants. He fears a similar danger may arise from the growing power of the commons. Voltaire employs the well-worn balance image to make the obvious point that in the Roman Republic there was no moderating influence to bring the warring plebeians and patricians into harmony, and he squarely charges the senators who kept all power in their hands with 'injuste et punissable orgueil', an aristocratic vice with which he had become only too well acquainted.

'Ce mélange heureux dans le gouvernement d'Angleterre, ce

concert entre les Communes, les Lords et le Roi' (IX, p.60): the
terms which Voltaire uses here to describe the English
constitutional balance suggest harmonious interaction and
collaboration even. They give no hint of the division of public
opinion, reflected in the periodical press of the time, over the
issue of the changing relations between the executive and
legislative powers of government. The full significance of the
change which was taking place was only dimly apprehended at
the time by the main participants in English political life and
seems to have eluded Voltaire altogether. The spokesman for the
Tory and Independent Whig opposition cried out in *The
Craftsman* against the innovations of Walpole's administration
which were subverting the constitution: 'the modern use of
cabinet-councils which is a device of foreign extraction' and the
impertinent 'notion of a prime-minister'. The fluidity in
governmental practice produced by the Hanoverian succession
was underlined in the effective shift of executive power
(unwarranted in the eyes of the Opposition) from an acquiescent
monarch to the leading figure among his servants. The prime
minister was responsible to the king, as were all his ministers,
but all ministers were answerable to parliament too. The
Opposition called for a king who would not only reign but
govern the country. The chief minister's main preoccupation
was to create and retain a majority to support him in parliament.
One answer to this problem lay in the assumed duty of the prime
minister (as against the crown) to dispense places and sinecures
in the King's Household — positions to which political strings
were invariably attached. The Opposition denounced the
plethora of pensions and 'place-men' produced by this bare-
faced corruption. It was stoutly defended by the governmental
faction as a 'laudable and necessary expedient of government'
however and indeed has been seen since by many historians as a
powerful factor in promoting the growth of political stability. In
deploring the 'corrupt dependency of the parliament on the
crown' the Opposition to Walpole could hardly have foreseen
that it would result not in the death of the constitution but in its
renewal. Voltaire may be suspected of wishing to run with the
hare and the hounds on this issue. He does not press the charge

of corruption and presents the apparatus of government in neutral terms, refraining from comment on the way in which it was used by politicians.

It was left to Montesquieu (another diligent reader of *The Craftsman*) to extrapolate and create a doctrine from the Opposition's demand for the mutual independence of the legislative and executive powers. Voltaire was more concerned with the constitutional trinity of king-in-parliament which made up one branch of government in England: the legislature. The balanced relationship of the three elements of the legislature in practice is described in Letter VIII. The king certainly appears as a 'sur-arbitre' in financial legislation and the balance is preserved. It was the wish of the Opposition that the monarch should remain above politics but by choosing his ministers exclusively from the dominant Whig party and giving them a free hand, it was felt that he was weakening the executive arm of government and the foundations of the constitution. 'Ministerial despotism' was, they pointed out, the result — supported by corruption in all forms, including not only the oiling of the parliamentary machine through the provision of lucrative posts but also the more brazen greasing of palms. Voltaire's eulogy of the British constitution would have pleased his various hosts whatever their political persuasion: 'ce gouvernement sage où le Prince, tout-puissant pour faire du bien, a les mains liées pour faire le mal, où les seigneurs sont grands sans insolence et sans vassaux, et où le peuple partage le gouvernement sans confusion' (VIII, p.55).

The supporters of Walpole who wrote for *The London Journal* stressed the 'mutual dependency' of the parts of the constitution. Voltaire likewise recognises the wise provision of checks and balances, but he stresses above all the cohesion and interdependence of the parts of the mechanism. There is no indication that he shared the Opposition view that, 'tout-puissant pour faire du bien' as he was, the Hanoverian monarch did not make enough use of the executive power which was his sole prerogative. Nor, it would appear, did he feel that a king with 'les mains liées pour faire le mal' was bound by anything other than the traditional restrictions of not being able to suspend the laws and of being tied to parliament as far as his income, his army, and the responsibility of his ministers were concerned. The development of the Cabinet represented a new form of limitation of royal power, but the advantage it produced in smoothness and efficacy of operation seems to have outweighed in Voltaire's eyes the possibly illusory disadvantages urged by those who interpreted the constitution in terms of the essential separation and independence of the spheres of action of its working parts.

Most of Letter IX is taken up with feudal and pre-feudal times when England did not enjoy the freedom arising from the harmonious and balanced relationship between king, lords and commons. In Voltaire's analysis of English history the flame of liberty, burning bright under the Hanoverians, had only begun to glimmer in the Dark Ages as a result of the power-struggle between the king and the lords of his kingdom. Magna Carta, regarded by Englishmen as a beacon in the history of freedom in their country, for Voltaire only serves to highlight their continued subjection to tyranny. The emergence of the commons as a real force does not take place until the beginning of the sixteenth century, and it is facilitated again by the clash of royal and baronial interests. The policies of Henry VII and Henry VIII brought about a shift in the balance of power. The people, with the end of feudal tenures, eagerly bought and exploited the lands relinquished by feckless overlords, whose numbers had soon to be kept up by the creation of peerages with no landed estates attached. The development of the institutions of government is intimately related to this economic development in Voltaire's view of the history of parliament.

This view is opposed to the dominant Whig interpretation of the history of the English people. Throughout the eighteenth (and much of the nineteenth) century, the idea that the institutions of England had been free from time immemorial was an integral part of this tradition. *The Craftsman*, which may be taken as a typical exponent of the tradition, presents a picture of ancient Britons imbued with a 'love of civil liberty' resisting the Saxons, who far from giving up the freedom of their Gothic institutions set up a system of government with 'the supreme power centred in the wicklemote or wittenagemote, composed of the king, lords and the Saxon freemen, that original sketch of a British parliament'. Voltaire, in characteristically demystifying fashion, dismisses this version of history as a naively jingoistic distortion of the brutal fact of age-old oppression of the silent unrepresented majority by their rapacious masters. He comes very near to *The Craftsman*'s narrative when he introduces a domineering clergy alongside the kings and barons, and even surpasses its anti-clerical animus by tracing the tradition of clerical tyranny back to those precursors of the power-seeking prelates, the ancient Druids. His own view, as expressed in the *Letters Concerning the English Nation*, was that during the post-Conquest period 'the commonalty had little or no share in the legislature; made no figure in the government'.

The distinction between Whig and Tory was becoming blurred in the 1720s and the older division into Court and Country was adopted by the political opposition to Walpole. Voltaire, not wishing to antagonise potential readers on either side, trod carefully in this area. Broadly speaking, however, he is in instinctive sympathy with the forces representing the future rather than with the conservative politics of nostalgia associated with the Country attitude. Bolingbroke and his circle (Pope, Swift, Gay, Arbuthnot), anti-Walpole and pro-Country, rejected the old political party labels. The ideas they espoused — the myth of an ancient constitution safeguarding popular representation, the idea that the laws and parliament of the seventeenth century were immemorial and merely confirmed by the Revolution of 1688 — were part of the legacy of the Whigs. The journalists in Walpole's pay ignored this legacy and took up the arguments of the seventeenth-century Tory, Robert Brady, who denied the antiquity of the Commons and stressed the monopoly of power enjoyed by the barons and the church under a feudal system which had no place for freeholders. They presented the Revolution as a radical new departure. It would seem therefore that Voltaire's account of the slow and difficult emergence of parliamentary institutions owes as much to Walpole's hacks as to his friend Bolingbroke.

The second half (roughly) of Letter IX is concerned with land

and the growth of what was to be called 'the landed interest'.
The freeholders, whose role in the political life of the country
begins with the end of feudalism in Voltaire's analysis,
exemplify the essential connection between 'liberty and
property', watchwords of the supporters of the Revolution. The
basis of the free institutions which Voltaire praises is the right to
own property and he sees the fundamental attitude of all English
citizens, high and low, as that of the proprietor. The situation
where the vast majority sowed for a tiny minority to reap the
benefits of their labour is viewed with repugnance, but his
observation that it has changed and that, with the end of
feudalism, justice has been rendered to humanity is surely
premature. The world of the 'labouring poor' in the England of
the 1720s was harsher than his picture of it would suggest. The
chaotic French legal system with its diverse forms of
jurisprudence is used as a point of comparison but it hardly
mitigates the defects of the English system. Voltaire's reference
to an enlightened England which knows nothing of the French
lord of the manor's exclusive right to hunt on his estate and its
adverse effects on the peasantry takes no account of the real
situation. The English game laws up to 1831 specifically
favoured men of rank and substance: hunting rights were
reserved for landowners and 'sons of persons of high degree',
who were allowed free access to game on other people's
property. And this in an age when offences against property
were regarded as extremely serious and punished severely. It is
true that an Englishman, as long as he was not poor, flaunted his
liberties and rejoiced in contrasting the French *lettre de cachet*
with his own country's 'habeas corpus', which meant he could
not be imprisoned without trial. To the poor man, unable to
raise the money for bail or avoid the debtor's prison, however,
this meant nothing. The two hundred or so offences for which
he could be hanged were of more importance. Neither the urban
nor the rural poor in fact find a place in Voltaire's picture. The
English 'peasant' whom he describes as being well-shod, well-
fed, well-dressed is also well-off and in a suitable position to
scorn the 'Popery and wooden shoes' which begin at Calais. It is
true that the peasants in France constituted 90% of the total

population and that there were bound to be more of them living on the bread-line than their English counterparts. All the same, Voltaire is not comparing like with like when he chooses to set a wealthy English freeholder, worth 200,000 livres (the contemporary equivalent of close on £9,000) against, by inference, a poor *fermier* rather than the more prosperous type of *laboureur* upon whom Molière modelled his George Dandin. It serves his polemical purpose also to show this English commoner who continues to work on his own land as an example of the ethic of work which brings (taxable) wealth. Although many an impoverished French *hobereau* of the minor nobility was forced to plough his own land, such an example would have done nothing to serve Voltaire's purpose of showing up the idleness of the French aristocrat. This letter shows him enjoying exemption from taxation by nature of his social rank, and the next one will show him a parasite at Versailles.

Letter IX ends with a reference to 'la terre qui les [i.e. les paysans] a enrichis'; the opening words of Letter X are 'Le commerce qui a enrichi les citoyens...'. The link between these two sources of wealth was a real one and was reflected at many points in British society in the eighteenth century. The traditional and still the prime source of wealth was land and the country gentry formed the backbone of English political life. In particular, the squire of rural England, as Justice of the Peace, was a key-figure in the country's judicial system. He was also a figure of importance in the whole scheme of local and national government, and was expected to exert his influence, by fair means or foul, to ensure the success of his patron's favoured candidate in elections to the House of Commons. Widespread bribery and corruption was as much a part of the political life of the urban justices, the aldermen and burgesses as of their country cousins. Voltaire's presentation of the government and society of Hanoverian England must appear painfully lacking in depth to the enquiring student of social history. The few venal members of the English parliament who receive his attention are but the tip of an iceberg, which he deliberately ignores or knows nothing about.

In any case, money was never regarded by Voltaire as the root

of all evil. As a canny speculator himself he was bound to be
alive, if not sympathetic, to the Country party's campaign
against the 'monied interest' and its constant denunciation of
the 'evils' of speculation and stock-jobbing. In Letter VIII,
Voltaire refers to England's quixotic involvement in costly
warfare on the Continent to illustrate, somewhat naively, her
almost incredible attachment to liberty; the second paragraph of
Letter X is similarly concerned with the War of the Spanish
Succession and the financial cost of land wars, but this time to
underline the increasingly important role of those who can
assure the money supply. The 'marchands anglais', whose aid
was directly responsible for the relief of Turin, in this instance
appear in the guise of bankers or financiers. Their wealth derives
from commerce but it is, we may note, their lending at interest
which elicits Voltaire's praise for their civic virtue. The
commerce which had made England rich and powerful, as he
points out, is her overseas trade based upon her maritime
supremacy. Voltaire's association of British sea-power with the
theme of liberty already catches the note which will be sounded
six years later in the song 'Rule Britannia'. The Country party's
distaste for the ruinous expense of military campaigns on land
and its 'blue-water' policy of supporting naval warfare in the
interests of national prosperity is evoked by Voltaire's image of
a nation, poor in national resources but otherwise resourceful in
her aggressive pursuit of trade and her determination to rule the
waves, above all else, in a mercantile sense.

It is evident that Voltaire's middle-class family background
leads him to share vicariously the 'juste orgueil' of the English
'marchand' or 'négociant' — terms which are interchangeable in
Letter X. The shadow of Rohan also looms large in this letter
which reflects the earlier view of the English nobility as being
'grands sans insolence' (Letter VIII). The arrogant and
pretentious French courtier is cut down to size and presented as
an automaton whose little life is measured out by the petty
routine of the King's daily round and bounded by the limited
horizon of a minister's ante-chamber. The English merchant
lives on a different plane, for he has complete freedom of
manœuvre to plan for the future and from his office his word

goes out to distant parts of the globe with important and
beneficial results. This international dimension of the
merchant's activity has been suggested in the first paragraph of
the letter with its evocation of overseas trading in the Baltic, the
Mediterranean and the Caribbean. The term 'merchant' covered
a wide variety of activities in the eighteenth century, ranging
from international trade, merchant banking and all the financial
dealings (stock jobbing, insurance, exchange, broking, etc.)
which are still connected with the City, down to wholesale and
retail trade on the internal market. Voltaire clearly has in mind
large-scale mercantile enterprise associated with the merchant
princes described as 'greater and richer and more powerful than
some sovereign princes' by Daniel Defoe in his, nowadays
confusingly titled, *Complete English Tradesman* (1725).
Representatives of the 'landed interest' inevitably mingled with
those of the 'monied interest': great landowners were interested
in foreign trade and invested their money in shipping, nobles
married their sons to the daughters of merchants and bankers,
and country gentlemen helped govern the country alongside
merchants on the bench at Quarter Sessions or in the House of
Commons. Voltaire chooses to illustrate the link between the
aristocracy and the merchant class in England by what he admits
is a dying practice: that of younger sons going into trade. His
choice springs, doubtless, from his desire to provide a strong
contrast between an England enlightened in its attitude to social
mobility, and what he seeks to expose as his own caste-ridden
country. In France a noble was debarred from engaging in
'ignoble', menial trade and risked losing his title and privileges if
he decided to *déroger* in this way. Commercial activity on a
grander scale — overseas trade, for example — was open to him
and officially encouraged from 1756. The social stigma
remained for the die-hard *noblesse de race* (as distinct from the
newly-ennobled) a strong deterrent, however, and it is this
stubborn aristocratic prejudice which Voltaire is chiefly
concerned to combat in his eulogy of the English merchant. His
animus against the impoverished but supercilious minor German
nobility (shades of *Candide* and Thunder-ten-tronckh) and the
breed of the newly-ennobled French snobs drives him to take up

the cause of the merchant of his own country who is, foolishly, too diffident to defend himself. There is a large element of wish-fulfilment in Voltaire's *plaidoyer* — to remind us again that his account of English society is polemical rather than objective.

The English merchant is presented, in Letter X, as being far more vocal in his aspirations than his French counterpart and surrounding himself (like 'M. Shipping' M.P. in Letter VIII) with that same aura of respectability which attaches to the ancient Romans. It may well be that Voltaire was influenced and misled to some extent by his host Fawkener and his Huguenot friends in the business world in his assessment of the general esteem in which merchants, whether in a big or small way of business, were held in England. His own personal experience, to judge from his private note-books, made him aware of the difficulty of becoming accepted on a social level in England. It would have required little extra imaginative effort on his part to arrive at the plain truth that in England, no less than in France, it took three generations for a merchant's family to become fully assimilated and accepted by the social group into which it gained entry. It does not seem unwarrantable to assume that Voltaire's solidarity with the aims and ambitions of the English merchant is not based entirely upon the latter's self-evaluation. He fully deserves a place in the movement of glorification, on both sides of the Channel, of those engaged in commerce. The parallelism and often interaction between English and French currents of thought is made strikingly evident in the way in which Voltaire in Letter VI borrows from Addison's *Spectator* the image of the Stock Exchange. He kills two birds with one stone by showing business being amicably transacted between men of different creeds (in place of Addison's different nationalities) and thus emphasising religious toleration as well as the secular values of utility and prosperity fostered by the commercial spirit. Lillo's *London Merchant* (1731) anticipates Voltaire's letter 'Sur le commerce' in its praise of mercantilism as a factor in international peace and prosperity and John Gay's *The Distress'd Wife* (1734), whilst making clear the condescending attitude still taken towards the merchants by much of English society, points to commerce as the foundation of Britain's international reputation and power. In France, Sedaine in his *Philosophe sans le savoir* (1756) will offer a picture, familiar to readers of the *Lettres philosophiques*, of the merchant as 'un homme qui d'un trait de plume se fait obéir d'un bout de l'univers à l'autre'. Later on in the century Beaumarchais in his *Les Deux Amis* (1770) will represent the 'négociant' in the same light as in the tenth of the *Lettres philosophiques*: a Voltairean anti-hero, a diligent citizen working for the happiness, peace and prosperity of his fellow-countrymen: 'Au moment que le guerrier se repose, le négociant a le bonheur d'être à son tour l'homme de la patrie' (Act II, Scene 10).

To devote an entire letter to the practice of inoculation might seem curious on Voltaire's part. The subject appears at first sight as an example of English eccentricity in line with the national reputation for melancholia and suicide. That this 'coutume étrange' is presented with an overriding polemical intent is soon evident, however, and it is the mad dogs, the English, who show up their French neighbours as 'd'étranges gens' and are ranged, in the final clinching example, with the Chinese as the depositaries of wisdom. Inoculation is associated with a whole range of enlightened values which, on Voltaire's showing, England shares. First of all, the commercial spirit lauded in the previous letter is evoked indirectly by the Middle Eastern locale: Circassia recalls the earlier references to Aleppo, Surat and Cairo. More directly, the Circassians are a trading people motivated by enlightened self-interest: 'Une nation commerçante est toujours fort alerte sur ses intérêts, et ne néglige rien des connaissances qui peuvent être utiles à son négoce' (XI, p.71). The main traffic (a term frequently used as a synonym for trade in eighteenth-century England) in which the Circassians engage is, undeniably, human lives; the opportunity of using the slave-trade to jolt his readers out of their instinctive reaction of repugnance and into a more rational attitude is persuasively exploited by Voltaire. Venial sins of the flesh were often taken by him as the occasion for slightly ribald humour. 'Un petit mal pour un grand bien', which sums up how the marital infidelity of the heroine of a Voltairean *conte* is presented in a broader ethical perspective, is certainly applicable to inoculation, but also to the training of the prospective harem-dwellers. Voltaire's utilitarianism foreshadows the appearance of Jeremy Bentham's doctrine of 'the greatest happiness of the greatest number' in the nineteenth century. The numerous attempts which were made in eighteenth-century England to devise a 'felicific calculus' to quantify happiness are reflected in the eleventh of the *Lettres philosophiques* in the use of rough and ready statistics in the final paragraphs to make a demographic point. More straightforwardly, the idea that life was for the living, here and now, was axiomatic for a hedonist like Voltaire and it is the life-enhancing property of inoculation, its capacity to preserve the precious gift of physical beauty, as well as its power to save human lives, which he stresses. In all this, progressive England comes out well in comparison with a backward France. The empiricism which will be distinguished in the following letters as the distinctive British contribution to the history of philosophy is here shown in Lady Mary Wortley Montagu's resolute attachment to the experimental method. Her maternal tenderness is in no way impugned ('L'expérience ne pouvait pas manquer de réussir'), and in her 'bienfaisance' (one of the Enlightenment's key concepts), she is yoked with the embodiment of another Enlightenment ideal in the person of the future Queen of England, Caroline, then Princess of Wales, who is described as 'née pour encourager tous les arts et pour faire du bien aux hommes; c'est un philosophe aimable sur le trône' (XI, p.72). Caroline as a benefactor of humanity, certainly has something in common with 'les grands hommes' whom Voltaire in the letters that follow installs in his personal pantheon, even if she is not on a par with them.

The final paragraph of Letter XI raises the debate on inoculation to a higher level by shifting the ideological ground from the terrain of the 'Europe chrétienne' of the opening sentence with its narrow Judeo-Christian frame of historical reference to a civilisation which is untainted by organised religion and of much greater antiquity. It marks the culmination of the attack against the obscurantist, anti-scientific world-view which has been conducted earlier in the letter and it looks forward to Voltaire's final remarks on Pascal's *Pensées*.

(iii) *Philosophy and Science*

Towards the end of his letter on Locke, Voltaire offers the reader this sobering thought:

> Divisez le genre humain en vingt parts: il y en a dix-neuf composées de ceux qui travaillent de leurs mains, et qui ne sauront jamais s'il y a un Locke au monde; dans la vingtième partie qui reste, combien trouve-t-on peu d'hommes qui lisent! Et parmi ceux qui lisent, il y en a vingt qui lisent des romans, contre un qui étudie la philosophie. Le nombre de ceux qui pensent est excessivement petit...

In his survey of English philosophy and science, he is writing about an élite and for an élite. Among the 'petit troupeau' of *philosophes* referred to earlier (VII, p.51) he had mentioned Newton, Clarke, Locke and Le Clerc. In Letter XIII (p.88) the roll-call comprises Montaigne, Locke, Bayle, Spinoza, Hobbes, Shaftesbury, Collins and Toland. What all these philosophers are said to have in common is lack of appeal for the mass of the reading public. Although his analysis is applied to 'le genre humain' as a whole, Voltaire nevertheless appears to regard the English as an exception. We are told in Letter XX (p.132) 'En Angleterre communément on pense'. The same idea is expressed in the notebook he kept during his stay in England: 'We have begun in France to write pretty well, before we have begun to think. English on the contrary'. In a notebook which post-dates the publication of the *Lettres philosophiques* there is a similar remark: 'D'où vient que les Italiens sont de si mauvais philosophes, et de si fins politiques, les Anglois au contraire?' When Voltaire notes, during his stay, that 'An Englishman is full of taughts' (i.e. thoughts), the context makes it clear that it is not the intellectual acumen of the man in the street which is in question, but the blunt and incisive way in which he expresses his opinion. 'Les Anglais approchent plus des Romains que nous, ils pensent et nous parlons', he noted later. It is no accident that this 'nation of philosophers' (D303), plain-spoken and down-to-earth, should have produced a tradition of philosophy which reflects in more refined form the rugged virtues of the national character. This aspect of Voltaire's view of England needs to be considered next; other aspects of the 'philosophic' content of Letters XII-XVII will receive attention in a later chapter.

Empiricism — the doctrine that all knowledge derives from experience — has been the dominant tradition in British philosophy since the seventeenth century. An empirical approach to the study of the natural world basing itself on experiment and observation was favoured by the great English scientists of that century. The impressive results of their work led other thinkers to apply the scientific method to a broader concern with man and society.

Voltaire is not distorting intellectual history unduly when he devotes three of the letters exclusively to Newton and another to a comparison between Descartes and the English scientist. Newton's pre-eminent role in the seventeenth-century revolution was certainly appreciated by his contemporaries. Locke's *Essay Concerning Human Understanding* (1690) is prefaced by an 'Epistle to the Reader' in which 'the incomparable Mr. Newton' is highly placed among the 'masterbuilders, whose mighty designs in advancing the sciences will leave lasting monuments to posterity'. Locke modestly proposes a humbler role for himself 'as an under-labourer in clearing the ground a little, and removing some of the rubbish that lies in the way of knowledge'. His positive contribution to philosophy, which he defines as 'nothing but the true knowledge of things', was a new view of how one acquires such knowledge. The scientist is concerned with the discovery of objective facts; the philosopher directs his attention to the human mind and investigates its workings in a scientific spirit. Locke's inquiry leads to the conclusion that all our ideas derive from sense-experience. Simple ideas come directly from sense-impressions; complex ideas are indirectly built up from simple ideas by reflection. This active role of the mind in using simple ideas as building-blocks was discarded when Locke's thought was imported into France. The thirteenth *lettre philosophique* represents one stage in the influence of Locke's theory of knowledge upon the development of the

French Enlightenment. Condillac's presentation of the mind in his *Traité des sensations* (1754) as merely a passive receptacle of sense-impressions distorted Locke's sensationalism. Voltaire's case against Cartesian innate ideas, with its suggestion that God's omnipotence could extend to endowing matter with thought, did not. He deserves the credit for the popularisation of this influential current of English thought in a state of relatively pristine purity. He was to regret, as much as Locke would have done, its subsequent transformation into the atheistic materialism of *philosophes* like Helvétius and d'Holbach.

'The application of experimental philosophy to moral subjects': this is the basis of 'the science of man' with which the most illustrious of British empiricists, David Hume, is concerned in his *Treatise of Human Nature*, which he wrote in France over the period 1734-1737. Already in 1733, it should be remembered, Voltaire in his *Letters Concerning the English Nation* had presented empiricism as the most significant tradition in English thought. Hume's introduction to his *Treatise* concurs with Voltaire's view and also singles out Bacon as the father of experimental philosophy and the forerunner of those *philosophes* (with Locke outstanding among them) who 'have begun to put the science of man on a new footing'. The *Lettres philosophiques* do not, of course, aim to explore methodically the possible merits of applying the experimental method to the study of epistemology, psychology, ethics and sociology. They do, however, echo continually the concern with human relations and particularly human happiness which underlines empirical investigation in all these fields.

Voltaire's presentation of English thought is as selective, and often as simplified, as his treatment of other aspects of English life. The Bacon-Newton-Locke filiation which makes up the central strand of these six letters clearly establishes Voltaire's own philosophical stance. Descartes is shown as a pioneer who prepared the way for Newton but his view of the physical universe, totally incompatible with 'la philosophie expérimentale', is rejected. His critical attitude towards tradition and authority and his belief in the value of free intellectual inquiry however are commended. He is ranged alongside the English philosophical trio for having contributed to the destruction of the mediaeval scholastic philosophy ('la misérable philosophie de l'Ecole', XIV, p.92) which was an amalgam of Aristotle and Christian theology quite foreign to empirical principles, but his attachment to hypotheses did not conform to Newtonian orthodoxy and so put him out of favour with Voltaire. Descartes's rationalism is condemned only insofar as it is, from the empiricist's point of view, misdirected. The construction of an all-embracing system of knowledge of man and the world on the basis of deductive reasoning from intuitively perceived general principles was denounced by the opponents of Cartesianism. Voltaire shared their distaste for this 'esprit systématique qui aveugle les plus grands hommes' (XIII, p.83) and their belief that true knowledge could only be acquired by inductive reasoning from premises firmly based on experience or experimental evidence. The positive aspect of Descartes's rationalism, its surging confidence in man's power to dominate his physical environment, is echoed in the buoyancy of the empiricists' faith in the advantages which scientific progress can bring to mankind. The philosophical modesty of Locke, the cautiousness of Newton bring hard-won but real gains instead of more easily amassed but illusory assets.

Voltaire's experience of England will ensure his abiding concern with limited and realistic objectives within the reach of ordinary humanity. The letters on philosophy and science are primarily concerned with analysing the English contribution to the 'advancement of learning' (to use Bacon's phrase). The distinctive contribution to the sum of human knowledge made by this 'nation of philosophers' is adjudged to be more important than its record in the field of human conflict, political or military. Those of her citizens who have spread enlightenment by increasing man's understanding of the world in which he lives are not to be compared with the inferior breed of politicians and conquerors, the 'illustres méchants' whose fame rests on human misery (XII, p.76). England's glory is enhanced by the dispassionate search for truth which has engaged the great minds of some of her thinkers and resulted in discoveries which have changed man's views of the world. It is interesting that although Voltaire glorifies peaceful intellectual inquiry, he makes a point of distinguishing the results of such disinterested research from the numerous useful inventions which have proved so beneficial to mankind: 'Les inventions les plus étonnantes et les plus utiles ne sont pas celles qui font le plus d'honneur à l'esprit humain' (XII, p.78). Here one sees how his original project had been modified. The 1728 *Advertisement*'s 'new inventions or undertakings, which have obtained or deserved success' in England are no longer a preoccupation, however useful they may be to his fellow-countrymen. Voltaire is offering his readers something more ambitious: an exercise in intellectual history, the story of the progress of the human mind in its journey from the scholastic philosophy of the Dark Ages towards 'des temps bien plus éclairés' (XII, p.78). The key role of English experimentalism — 'la saine philosophie' (XII, p.79) — in determining the evolution of the French Enlightenment is already being presented in the *Lettres philosophiques* as a chapter in the history of ideas.

In a letter of 1736 Voltaire describes Isaac Newton as 'le plus grand homme qui ait jamais été, mais le plus grand, de façon que les géants de l'antiquité sont auprès de lui des enfants qui jouent à la fossette' (D1174). In his account of English science in the *Lettres philosophiques*, Newton's towering genius is presented in the same terms. He is 'un homme...tel qu'il s'en trouve à peine en dix siècles' (XII, p.76), whose prodigious achievements in geometry and physics have opened up an entirely new vista of an infinite universe, besides which the hitherto plausible Cartesian world must appear arbitrary and incredible. His life's work was recognised at home by burial in Westminster Abbey, the sort of final respects normally reserved for a king. Abroad he acquired 'une réputation si universelle' (XV, p.96) that Voltaire wonders if the value of his investigation of the chronological foundations of the study of history will be under-rated by jealous scholars loath to allow Newton's mastery in yet another field to establish his claim to 'une espèce de monarchie universelle'.

In the four letters devoted to Newton, Voltaire's posture is that of the humble and reverential layman in the presence of an unparalleled example of scientific genius. The tone of his remarks is one of constant wonderment at 'l'effort de la finesse et de l'étendue de l'esprit humain' (XVII, p.113) which has pierced seemingly inpenetrable mysteries of the physical universe and then revealed these secrets in plain and simple language. His own aim is to analyse these discoveries with the same lucidity for his readers and to convey the importance of the scientific method which produced them. 'Je vais vous dire', he says, '(si je puis, sans verbiage) le peu que j'ai pu attraper de toutes ces sublimes idées' (XV, p.96). His promised attempt to keep his exposition succinct and free from jargon is strikingly successful. His ready admission of superficiality, however, needs to be borne in mind.

Voltaire's interest in Newton had probably been aroused before his visit to England. The exiled Bolingbroke wrote to Pope early in 1724 that his home was a hive of intellectual activity shared by two close companions: Voltaire and Lévesque de Pouilly. Pouilly had been one of the editors of *L'Europe savante*, a learned journal which had been a focus for debate between Cartesians and Newtonians in 1718, and his thorough grounding in Newtonian ideas was acknowledged. Voltaire recognised this special expertise: referring to Pouilly's primacy as a Newtonian he wrote in 1738: 'Je n'ai que le mérite d'avoir osé effleurer le premier en public, ce qu'il eût approfondi s'il eût voulu' (D1558). The fifteenth *lettre philosophique* echoes the Newton-Descartes debate in *L'Europe savante* between 'attractionnaires' supporting the vacuum and denouncing the abuse of hypotheses, and 'impulsionnaires' vindicating the plenum and deriding the force of gravity as a scholastic 'occult quality'.

Bolingbroke's contribution to any discussion of Newton can be guessed at from the contemptuous remarks about Cartesian physics in an important letter of June 1724 (D190). During Voltaire's visit to England, however, it was probably his personal contact with Dr Samuel Clarke (see Letter VII), who expounded to him the theological implications of Newton's thought, which stimulated him to study Newton's physics later.

The real fruits of this study are apparent not in the *Lettres philosophiques* but in the later *Eléments de la philosophie de Newton* (1740). Voltaire had become a convinced Newtonian through the influence of Maupertuis in 1732, but his Newtonianism is based not on a thorough acquaintance with Newton's work so much as upon a sound general appreciation of the English scientist's contribution to knowledge. This appreciation is what we have in Letters XIV-XVII.

(iv) *Literature and the Arts*

Voltaire offers himself as a reliable guide to the literary scene in contemporary England. He takes pains to establish his authority and his right to criticise earlier commentators like Béat de Muralt (XIX, p.126) and Saint-Evremond (XXI, p.136). A remark he makes about English comedy is obviously meant to present his credentials: 'Si vous voulez connaître la comédie anglaise, il n'y a d'autre moyen pour cela que d'aller à Londres, d'y rester trois ans, d'apprendre bien l'anglais et de voir la comédie tous les jours' (XIX, p.129). Yet, however thorough his immersion in the intellectual and cultural atmosphere of the country might have been, it could never have guaranteed his total impartiality as an observer. His admiration for English liberty did not extend to abandoning his literary taste which had been formed in all essentials during his schooldays by his reading of the masterpieces of French classicism. He could not condone English disregard for the formal discipline of composition, for those hallowed rules and conventional proprieties which only served to enhance the artistic impact of a work in the hands of a Racine. Besides being a man of taste in the neoclassical mould, however, Voltaire was also a man of feeling if ever there was one. He responded powerfully to any appeal to his emotions and he was faint in his praise of any work which failed to move him. His life-long adherence to 'le bon goût universel' never altered his over-riding attachment to the unformulated but most important rule of all: never bore your audience. The unfamiliarly bizarre and grotesque elements in English literature went against the neoclassical grain but they were bound to appeal to 'la curiosité d'un homme raisonnable' (I, p.20), i.e. to Voltaire and also to his French readers. These readers would find an accurate reflection of their own taste in Voltaire's view of the Restoration period as a high point in English cultural history, 'l'âge d'or des beaux-arts' (XVIII, p.121), and in his favourable critical assessment of those English writers of the next century whose work enshrined unexceptionable neoclassical values. More interesting for readers of today, and possibly for many of his own day, however, are Voltaire's still freshly personal reactions to what captured his interest and imagination.

Some striking products of the English creative imagination — 'le génie poétique des Anglais' (XVIII, p.124) — are what Voltaire primarily wants to display in this section of the *Lettres philosophiques*. This aim is part of a broader aspiration to promote greater awareness of national culture on each side of the Channel and to encourage cross-fertilisation between writers working within different traditions and conventions. This ideal, strikingly realised by Voltaire himself in his debts to English practice in plays like *La Mort de César* (1736), had been embodied first of all in his essay on European epic poetry and is clearly articulated in the final paragraph of Letter XXII, which could be seen as dimly foreshadowing the later concept of comparative literature.

There is a decidedly disarming quality about his determination (announced in Letter XVIII, p.121) to look for virtues rather than defects in the authors he treats. His genuine enthusiasm, however, is reserved for what he regards as highlights, 'des lueurs étonnantes' (XVIII, p.123) amid the prevailing gloom. This results in a highly selective survey, focused upon certain 'endroits frappants' or 'morceaux détachés' (XVI, pp.121, 123), very freely translated for the most part, and with many additions which serve Voltaire's polemical intentions at the expense of the original and often seem to be included for that purpose rather than for their representative or intrinsic value. Intermittent attempts are made to identify the distinctive features of 'le génie poétique des Anglais', but its relation to the general spirit of freedom animating all aspects of English life remains implicit.

Voltaire prefers to single out specific authors and works for explicit comment. His choices are fairly arbitrary and his coverage of this restricted range of literary activity very uneven. First of all, one is struck by the often curious omissions. Milton, whose work Voltaire may justifiably claim to have introduced to France, receives no mention. The conspicuous absence of any consideration of prose fiction leaves Defoe out in the cold. Restoration comedy is treated at some length, but although Congreve, Vanburgh and Wycherley are neatly characterised, the bulk of Letter XIX is taken up with plot-summaries. Molière as a source of some of the plays discussed hovers in the background throughout this letter as a legitimate point of reference. The comparative approach is not so successful in other letters: Voiture receives inordinate attention in Letter XXI through being compared with the equally insignificant Waller; little light is shed upon the poetry of Swift by the elucidation of his reputation as 'le Rabelais d'Angleterre' (XXII, pp.142-43).

The subjective bias of the view of English literature presented in the *Lettres philosophiques* is evident in the subject-matter of the translated extracts. Voltaire's initial preoccupation with the proverbially suicidal melancholia of his English hosts may be related not only to Hamlet's sombre ruminations on self-slaughter (XVIII, p.122), but also to Dryden's pessimistic thoughts on the human condition (XVIII, pp.122-23) and, above all, to the translation of the lines from Pope's *Rape of the Lock* which deal with the 'gloomy cave of Spleen'. Rochester, surely no-one's automatic choice for the pantheon of English letters, is introduced as 'l'homme de génie et le grand poète' less for his real worth as a poet, one feels, than for his anti-clerical sentiments (XXI, p.137). Hervey, the unnamed 'seigneur anglais' inaccurately described as 'fort jeune', is similarly acclaimed for a vigorous rejection (XX, p.133) of religious inertia which sounds a stirringly activist note, harmonising with the work's general philosophical tenor to which Voltaire's more intimate, darker moods provide a muted counterpoint.

Natural vigour, impatient with the formal constraints of versification and the requirements of polite society, constituted, for Voltaire, Rochester's strength as a poet. This spirit of

freedom he felt to be the essential characteristic of English
literature, its compelling genius. Its polar opposite, a restrained
good taste, was the hall-mark of French culture. The opposition
between the two cultures is reflected throughout Voltaire's
career as a literary critic. The *Lettres philosophiques*, whilst
foreshadowing the later dominance of Voltaire's neoclassical
sympathies, mark the high point of his admiration for English
works and authors. Certainly, the Frenchified court of Charles
II is presented as a salutary cultural influence. The literature to
which this influence gave rise is seen as reflecting the wholly
desirable spread of social refinement and enlightened critical
values. These values were shared by the intellectual élite of
contemporary England from whom Voltaire frequently takes his
cue. This Anglo-French consensus of critical opinion is
represented in Letter XXII by Pope and Swift, exemplars of the
classical aesthetic of reason, clarity, discrimination and good
taste. Voltaire's unquestionable adherence to these basic
principles is tempered, however, by his appreciation of
specifically national traits. If his highest praise is reserved for
the universal appeal of Pope, his attraction to the impenetrably
English and inimitable Swift is also strikingly evident (p.143).
'Le sage Addison', disastrously imitable, has all the neoclassical
virtues but lacks the vital spark, whereas Dryden falls below
Voltaire's standards when judged by the touchstone of good
taste but wins praise for the vigour of his verse (XVIII, pp.122-
23). As for the supreme example of the undisciplined 'génie
poétique des Anglais', there is no doubt about Voltaire's choice
nor about his positive enthusiasm which he conveys in
appropriately hyperbolic terms: 'Les monstres brillants de
Shakespeare plaisent mille fois plus que la sagesse moderne'
(XVIII, p. 124).

Shakespeare is presented to the reader of the *Lettres
philosophiques* as the founding father of the English theatre, a
mighty genius whose awesome example continues to inspire
futile emulation in lesser writers. His prodigious gifts clearly put
him on a par with an intellectual giant like Pascal in Voltaire's
eyes. Sublime though both these 'forces de la nature' may be,
however, they are not immune from criticism. Culture may be

urged against nature, taste against genius. Voltaire had never wavered in the opinion which he offered to an English visitor in 1776 that 'Shakespeare had an amazing genius but no taste'. Just as Pascal's mysticism puts him out of court when judged by Voltaire's social conscience, Shakespeare is placed firmly beyond the pale for his ignorance of the critical guide-lines dictated by a refined society. The charge-sheet is extensive: breaking social barriers and standards of public decorum by introducing tippling grave-diggers and punning cobblers into the ostensibly aristocratic genre of tragedy, simulating bloodshed and violent death on stage, using strong language tainted with the figurative features of Biblical style ('l'enflure asiatique', XVIII, p.123), and showing no respect for order and discipline in the fundamental craft of composition. The pleasure which Shakespeare had given Voltaire the playgoer was bound to earn him some leniency however; as long as the sublime moments of high drama vibrated in the memory, the ridiculous episodes of low farce could be forgotten and even forgiven. Diminished responsibility is invoked and the general temper of the times is blamed for the low tone of Shakespearian tragedy. Voltaire has the *Lettres philosophiques* in mind when he writes, near the end of his life, in his *Lettre à l'Académie française* (1777): 'Je fus le premier qui tirai un peu d'or de la fange où le génie de Shakespeare avait été plongé par son siècle'.

For these pearls of concentrated tragic emotion produced by Shakespeare's native genius, one had to search in the dung-heap, as Voltaire put it, of grotesque concessions which he made to the age in which he lived. Voltaire did not, however, confine his attentions to the genius of Shakespeare and dismiss all else in him. There were other attractions. The love-interest imported from France by Restoration drama which had become regarded as an indispensable ingredient of all new plays was anathema to Voltaire. Shakespeare, with his *Julius Caesar*, offered an alternative model: political drama, devoid of *galanterie* and dealing with matters of high seriousness. Voltaire took it up, first of all in his *Brutus* (1731) and later in *La Mort de César* (1736). *Othello*, 'pièce très touchante' (XVIII, p.120) is often seen as an influence on his *Zaïre* (1732), whilst the appearance of

the ghost in *Eriphyle* in the same year may be attributed to the
apparition of Hamlet's father. The idea of French drama
strongly profiting from that of less sophisticated neighbours
always appealed to Voltaire. 'Leur théâtre est resté dans une
enfance grossière et le nôtre a acquis trop de raffinement. J'ai
toujours pensé qu'un heureux et adroit mélange de l'action qui
règne sur le théâtre de Londres et de Madrid, avec la sagesse,
l'élégance, la noblesse, la décence du nôtre pourrait produire
quelque chose de parfait', he wrote in 1764 in a tailpiece to his
translation into French of the first three acts of Shakespeare's
Julius Caesar. This cosmopolitan credo echoes the defence of
enlightened literary borrowing which closes the twenty-second
lettre philosophique.

On the whole, it would seem that Voltaire correctly recognised
the unique status of Shakespeare in the annals of English
literature. His claim to success, if not primacy, in popularising
his work in France is solidly based. This base as seen in the
Lettres philosophiques was not particularly broad:
Shakespeare's comedies were a closed book to him, he had read
(in some cases seen) a handful of tragedies and history plays.
What appears to have impressed him most was the external
dynamics of the action and the emotive impact of the situations
rather than any weightier psychological aspects of character-
isation. This impression, as recorded, partly at least, in the
Lettres philosophiques, was among the deepest and most
important of all those arising from his contact with England.

The literary critic intermittently takes second place to the
professional man of letters in Voltaire's remarks on English
writing. The reader is prepared in this way for the twenty-third
and twenty-fourth *lettres philosophiques* which are directly
concerned with the social and economic context of literary
production, and the role and status of the writer in society. The
sociology of literature, as we would call it, is a subject dear to
Voltaire's heart. Related certainly to the writer's compulsive
preoccupation with his posthumous reputation, it is more
concerned with the public esteem and material rewards that he
should receive from his contemporaries. To Voltaire, England
appears as a shining example of munificence in state patronage

of the arts, a country where the things of the mind are properly respected through the system of recognising intellectual worth in terms of honorific and lucrative public office: 'En Angleterre communément on pense et les lettres y sont plus en honneur qu'en France' (XX, p.132). This general remark had been preceded in Letter XIX (ostensibly on English comedy) by the observation that Colley Cibber's rather grandiose title of Poet Laureate was not to be sniffed at when a substantial income and considerable perquisites went with it. In Letter XXIII the point is amplified and supported by other examples: Addison, Newton, Congreve, Prior, Swift. Voltaire's evocation of Crébillon *père* almost starving to death and the late, great Racine's son on the bread line serves by contrast to reinforce the idea of an incredibly enlightened England. The idyllic picture (XX, p.132) of high culture percolating down to a politically articulate citizenry steeped in the classics seeks the same effect by conveniently suppressing the awkward aspects of the system of pensions and placemen and the disturbing incidence of parliamentary and electoral corruption. Seemingly mesmerised by the alluring perspective of pecuniary reward, Voltaire glibly dismisses the religious discrimination suffered by Roman Catholics as a trifle compared with the distinction conferred on one of their number, Alexander Pope, in the shape of the fat sum he received for his translation of Homer.

Voltaire briskly disposes of English historians in the penultimate paragraph of Letter XXII by suggesting that the partisan approach to politics which they shared with all their compatriots had effectively prevented them from producing an impartial history of their country. The only dispassionate and reliable history of England, he notes, had been written by a Frenchman, Rapin de Thoyras. The implication is that his own account of England has been written with the objectivity of a foreigner and is equally trustworthy. Only a very unwary reader, however, would take everything in the *Lettres philosophiques* on trust. The polemical ardour which vitiates English historical writing infuses Voltaire's commentary on English life with a similar vigour. Personal preoccupations and prejudices colour his view of the arts in England. The confrontation between the chevalier de Rohan, the boorish philistine, and Voltaire (*ci-devant* Arouet) standing on his precarious dignity as a man of letters still reverberates in the eulogy of English peers for whom the pen is no less respectable than the sword. These noblemen live up to their high position and show a true sense of social responsibility by setting an example of civilised regard for humane values: 'Leurs ouvrages leur font plus d'honneur que leur nom' (XXI, p.139). The reverse was the case in France where the business of writing carried the same social stigma as trade and commerce and a noble disgraced himself if he regarded it as anything other than a frivolous pastime. This turning upside down of the principle of *noblesse oblige* was one of the ridiculous aspects of 'le sot orgueil' (XXI, p.139) which permeated the rigidly stratified society of the Ancien Régime.

Equally ridiculous in Voltaire's native land is the inconsistent attitude of authority towards the theatre. The contradictions arising from the alliance between throne and altar are mercilessly exposed, and their folly reinforced by the contrast between Prynne the fanatical Puritan campaigner against play-going and Charles I and his wife, as passionately attached to the theatre as Voltaire himself. Voltaire's deepest indignation, however, is reserved for what he clearly feels as the most odious feature of 'cette barbarie gothique qu'on ose nommer sévérité chrétienne' (XXIII, p.151): the excommunication of the entire acting profession. Mrs Oldfield buried with the great in Westminster Abbey for the distinction she had brought to this profession makes a striking contrast with the 'barbare et lâche injustice' (XXIII, p.149) perpetrated by the French in denying the famous actress Adrienne Lecouvreur a decent Christian burial. The *Lettres philosophiques* echo at several points the spirited condemnation of his fellow-countrymen which Voltaire had voiced in his poem *La Mort de mademoiselle Lecouvreur* (1730), where England's treatment of Mrs Oldfield ('la charmante Ophils') is used as an eloquent indictment of the French. The 'Welches', as Voltaire was to refer to his compatriots at their most unappealing, had a lot to learn from enlightened England:

C'est là qu'on sait tout dire, et tout récompenser;
Nul art n'est méprisé, tout succès a sa gloire.

The model meritocracy described in the third paragraph of the twenty-third *lettre philosophique* had already been announced rather sweepingly in the earlier work: 'Quiconque a des talents à Londres est un grand homme'.

As if to forestall the charge of excessive enthusiasm for all things English, Voltaire in his discussion of the organisation of scholarship firmly states his preference for the French way of doing things. The rigorously controlled, fiercely competitive system of entry to the Académie des Sciences appeals to him more than the altogether more casual dependence on personal recommendation and trust in the intellectual grape-vine. The English system seems to Voltaire to be blighted by a muddle-headed amateurism which has no part in the emergence of a genius like Newton. He feels that the activities of learned societies should be geared to the objectives of society as a whole. The earlier note of disparagement of mere inventions (XII, p.78) is here recalled only to be countered by his clear option for applied as distinct from pure, useful as opposed to speculative, research. It is ironic that after condemning the blinkered pedantry of some members of the Académie des Belles-Lettres, the letter ends not merely on a note of national pride in the French literary heritage but with a staunch defence of linguistic conservatism. Dismay can be the English reader's only reaction when Voltaire, extolling the neoclassical values of purity and correctness, can think of nothing reflecting more honour on and bringing more benefit to humanity than a wholesale editorial purge of the minor faults of the great writers of the age of Louis XIV.

3 *The Making of a* philosophe

The twenty-fifth *lettre philosophique* should not be dismissed as a mere afterthought on Voltaire's part with little or no organic relation to the preceding letters. Far from being barely germane to the material concerning England, it can be considered as the culmination of all the tendentious remarks made earlier. It gives a keen polemical cutting edge to the work and serves to draw many of the implications of Voltaire's specific views on English life into a tighter synthesis centred upon the general concerns of mankind. In sharpening the philosophical focus in this way, it could be said to enhance rather than detract from the unity of the work as a whole. The remarks on Pascal, said to be 'faites depuis longtemps' (XXV, p.160), are the fruit of a long and continuing meditation which dates back to the period just before Voltaire's visit to England. Voltaire took up again and completed in the summer of 1733 reflections which had merely been fructified, as had other preoccupations of his, by the English experience. His respect for the genius and eloquence of Pascal and his fundamental aversion to the odious picture of human nature painted by 'ce misanthrope sublime' (ibid.) can be seen in the epistle in the *Mercure de France* of September 1732 which already sets out the aim of Letter XXV:

> J'examine avec soin les informes écrits,
> Les monuments épars et le style énergique
> De ce fameux Pascal, ce dévot satirique;
> Je vois ce rare esprit trop prompt à s'enflammer;
> Je combats ses rigueurs extrêmes:
> Il enseigne aux humains à se haïr eux-mêmes;
> Je voudrais, malgré lui, leur apprendre à s'aimer.
> (Epître à Mlle de Malcrais)

In his letter on Bacon, Voltaire compares the failure of the

Chancellor's estimable *Moral Essays* to please his readers with the success of the more readable *Maximes* of La Rochefoucauld which could only offer a specious 'satire de la nature humaine'. Letter XXV, one feels, attempts to offer a view of human nature which is more optimistic than La Rochefoucauld's or Pascal's and which sustains the high moral and philosophical tone of the preceding letters. That he had this question of the coherence of the *Lettres philosophiques* very much in mind may be seen from his correspondence with Thieriot. He believes that the first two editions (English and French) of his 'lettres anglaises' were rather on the slight side and needed to be buttressed by additional material. He discards various frivolous suggestions made by Thieriot and makes the well-considered choice of the 'anti-Pascal' as being weightier and more in keeping with the nature of 'un ouvrage...où les choses philosophiques l'emportent de beaucoup sur celles d'agrément' (D631).

Among 'les choses philosophiques' which Voltaire saw as providing intellectual ballast, the subject of religion bulks largest. The work opens with a series of short, sharp attacks on selected targets in the first seven letters on religion and closes with an all-out attack on the foremost Christian apologist in what is the most substantial letter. In the interval there is not only a great deal of satirical sniping but also a determined attempt to sap the foundations of the enemy's position. The crucial importance of the thirteenth letter on Locke is that it uses the weapon of Lockean psychology to establish a reasonable religion in which belief in God is supported entirely by the evidence provided by our senses. The genius of Newton enabled him to use this evidence to offer mankind a new revelation of the earth and the heavens which fortified the natural religion professed by Voltaire. Against these forces of light, Pascal's emphasis on the mystical aspects of religious experience and his intense faith in a personal God are made to appear retrograde, incompatible with man's higher aspirations and potentialities. The straightforward ethical core of the Christian religion, wholly compatible with Voltaire's own rational secular humanism, is used as a reproach against those Christians like Pascal who are charged with smothering it beneath metaphysical subtleties: 'Le christianisme n'enseigne que la simplicité, l'humanité, la charité; vouloir le réduire à la métaphysique, c'est en faire une source d'erreurs' (R1, p.161). To Voltaire these appear as arbitrary accretions, ingenious products of a wrong-headed approach to religion, mere reeds which may be swept aside without harming the solid oak of the gospel of Jesus Christ (XXV, pp.160-61). It is these 'reeds' which he claims to be clearing away in Letter XXV. 'Déchirer la peau de Pascal sans faire saigner le christianisme': this is how he stated his objective in a letter of June 1733 (D617), which shows more concern for saving his own skin in the face of the inevitable clerical reaction to his abrasive remarks than for sparing Christianity further blows. He is nevertheless motivated by more than ignoble expediency in the final *lettre philosophique*. As in the previous letters, his positive vindication of cherished values matches the destructive zeal he deploys against what he sees as the forces of darkness.

Pascal is for Voltaire the supreme anti-*philosophe*, the epitome of reactionary resistance to progressive ideas. He is the powerful irritant in the process which makes the 'anti-Pascal' a positive exercise in self-definition for its author, an important stage in the emergence of the concept of the *philosophe* in the restricted sense which it acquired during the French Enlightenment. Distaste for the irrational (whether mystical or superstitious) character of religion is an essential attribute of the *philosophe*. The narrator, 'homme raisonnable' as he is, deplores the 'enthusiasm' of the Quakers and the effect which Fox has on the rabble. In Letter XIII (p.87), this point is underlined: 'Jamais les philosophes ne feront une secte de religion. Pourquoi? C'est qu'ils n'écrivent point pour le peuple, et qu'ils sont sans enthousiasme'. Pascal is taken to task for not appreciating the true character of the philosopher: 'Les philosophes n'ont point enseigné de religion; ce n'est pas leur philosophie qu'il s'agit de combattre. Jamais philosophe ne s'est dit inspiré de Dieu, car dès lors il eût cessé d'être philosophe, et il eût fait le prophète' (RII, p.161). Indeed he is so profoundly out of sympathy with the rational 'philosophic' mentality that he seems, as Voltaire presents him, to belong to an even more distant past than the first dawning of enlightenment in the seventeenth century. His attachment to riddle and paradox is redolent of the obscurity of mediaeval scholasticism. His acceptance of the Biblical view of the privileged place of the Jewish people in the development of humanity naturally appears blinkered to his critic whose *Essai sur les mœurs*, with its broader perspective of global history, is anticipated here in his recognition of the antiquity of Chinese civilisation (XI, p.74). The glorious role played by numerous individual thinkers in the growth of civilisation is consistently acknowledged by Voltaire, who stresses the opposition and hostility they had to overcome. The *philosophe* as martyr, as the object of envy, calumny and downright persecution (to a large extent a Voltairean self-portrait) is already evident in the pen-pictures of Socrates (RXXIX, p.176), Descartes harried by jealous Dutch philosophers and domineering scholastics, Bacon admired throughout Europe but prey to the malice of English courtiers, and Galileo (XIV, p.92), victim of the Inquisition, dying a lonely death surrounded by enemies. Pascal is not to be found among the ranks of these secular martyrs. He belongs to the host of those whose faith is blind to the virtues which qualify for membership of Voltaire's pantheon.

The idea of a philosophic élite fastidiously detached from sectarian strife and sharing the esoteric values of an international fraternity of intellectuals does not square with the notion of embattled *philosophes* deeply concerned with combatting the harm wrought upon a country by a repressive regime. The relative political freedom and religious toleration enjoyed by the English were benefits which could be won only by struggle in France. The general religious apathy of Hanoverian Britain reflected the calm aftermath of bitter national dissension and could not be compared with the quiescence of a downtrodden French population. The dead hand of the Roman Catholic Church above all inhibited the vigorous cultivation and enjoyment of the fruits of the earth which France had in abundance. In France, an outgoing, forward-looking attitude to life is stifled by an inert asceticism which perverts sane moral values. This pernicious life-denying outlook comes under direct

attack in Letter XXV, but there is a build-up to the final assault.
The 'translations' in Letters XX and XXI are meant to do more
than illustrate literary merits; they have an explosive philosophic
charge. The picture of a priest-ridden Italy in the 'translation' of
Lord Hervey (XX, p.133) underlines the absurdity of poverty
amidst plenty, of stagnation accepted in the pursuit of a
misguided conception of holiness through self-mortification and
contemplation. The higher dignitaries of the Church, 'd'illustres
fainéants', and the lower orders of the clergy 'priant Dieu par
oisiveté' are supine witnesses of a sorry economic decline.
Voltaire returns to the attack on 'ces dévots/Condamnés par
eux-mêmes à l'ennui du repos' in the translation of Rochester
(XXI, p.137). Pascal's aversion to the restless activity which was
part of Voltaire's nature and his attachment to the
contemplative ideal are already evoked here by 'Ce mystique
encloîtré, fier de son indolence'. Voltaire's condemnation of this
inertia ('Réveille-toi, sois homme, et sors de ton
ivresse./L'homme est né pour agir, et tu prétends penser!') is
echoed by his later remark on Pascal: 'L'homme est né pour
l'action, comme le feu tend en haut et la pierre en bas. N'être
point occupé et n'exister pas est la même chose pour l'homme'
(RXXIII, p.173). To someone born to act, as the sparks fly
upward, 'l'ennui du repos' was as intolerable as it proved to be
to Candide, prompted to express his creator's conviction in the
most memorable form of all: 'Il faut cultiver notre jardin'.

The twenty-second of Voltaire's remarks on Pascal's *Pensées*
sees man's natural God-given tendency to look to the future as
essential to his well-being. One can reap only what one sows.
The need to work so as to provide for one's future happiness is
the corner-stone of Voltaire's enlightened hedonism. Feckless
self-indulgence is condemned as 'fausse jouissance': it is foolish
to regard this world as 'un lieu de délices où l'on ne doit avoir
que du plaisir' (RVI, p.166). Austere self-denial is equally futile,
however, and the moderate enjoyment of life's pleasures is a
sensible goal. The foundation of this hedonistic ethic is the
sensationalism of Locke: 'Celui-là est actuellement heureux qui
a du plaisir et ce plaisir ne peut venir que du dehors. Nous ne
pouvons avoir de sensations ni d'idées que par les objets

extérieurs' (RXXXV, p.178). Man seeks pleasure and avoids pain: a realistic ethic must take into account man's ineradicable self-love and society should be organised so as to contrive that mutual benefits for all derive from each individual's self-regard. Voltaire agrees with Pascal that 'chacun tend à soi' but he does not conclude, as Pascal does, that 'la pente vers soi est le commencement de tout désordre en guerre, en police, en économie, etc.' (RXI, p.168). On the contrary, he believes that the passions are the driving forces of society (RIII, p.163) and that the dynamic of self-interest and free enterprise produces a flourishing commerce which is in the national interest. Hedonism takes on a social dimension in his concern for 'la félicité publique' (IX, p.60), and the utilitarian concept of the greatest happiness of the greatest number comes into play in his appreciation of the quite respectable standard of material welfare of the lower orders of English society. The phrases which he uses ('rendre justice à l'humanité', 'bonheur pour le genre humain') in his account of English social history (IX, p.62) express his satisfaction with the improvement in the living conditions of the common people. They show the continuity between the earlier letters and his campaign in Letter XXV to 'prendre le parti de l'humanité' against Pascal.

Pascal's preoccupations are other-worldly; Voltaire's are resolutely down-to-earth. A numerous, healthy and contented citizen-body totally incurious about an after-life and thoughtlessly enjoying the affluence of modern urban civilisation was a source of satisfaction for Voltaire, but caused Pascal pangs of existential anguish (RVI, p.165). Voltaire, too, would be brought to the brink of despair some twenty years later, and man's inhumanity to man would be presented in *Candide* as one of the most disturbing aspects of evil in the world. In the early 1730s, however, Voltaire remained optimistic. Man had his allotted place in the Great Chain of Being: 'Penser que la terre, les hommes et les animaux sont ce qu'ils doivent être dans l'ordre de la Providence, est, je crois, d'un homme sage' (RVI, p.166). 'Whatever is, is right', Pope opines in his *Essay on Man*, and Voltaire ('ce n'est point à nous d'oser interroger la Providence', RXIII, pp.169-70) naturally

finds himself in agreement. As for human nature, Voltaire was
not inclined at this stage of his life to plumb its unsavoury
depths. Man was neither a paragon of goodness nor
irremediably corrupt: he was 'mêlé de mal et de bien' (RIII,
p.163). The forbidding God of Jansenist theology who granted
salvation to barely one in a million souls tainted by original sin
was not likely to encourage belief in His existence. The positive
action of the repentant sinner who sought redemption through
good works meant nothing to Him. This conception of God was
repugnant to Voltaire's activist mentality. For him, God's plan
for mankind is revealed in the way that He has fashioned human
nature so that inactivity breeds boredom, which drives us to
action useful to ourselves and to others (RXXVI, p.174). The
greatness of God is manifest in all His works; Pascal's famous
wager simply demeans His divinity. Where Pascal is seized by
metaphysical dread before the vastness of the heavens and his
own failure to feel God's presence in the silence of the limitless
universe (RVI, p.165), Voltaire needs no other argument to
prove God's existence than the wonder of the natural universe
which conveys this truth to every one of man's senses. Newton
reduced his own grounds for belief in a God to the single
argument from design, the first line of the nineteenth Psalm:
'The heavens declare the glory of God'. Voltaire's exposition of
Newton's discoveries is permeated with the same wonderment at
the glory both of inanimate nature and of the achievement of
human intellect. Pascal's chilling picture of man alone in the
universe, forsaken and bewildered, 'sans savoir qui l'y a mis, ce
qu'il y est venu faire, ce qu'il y deviendra en mourant' (RVI,
p.165) is (in 1734, at least) in stark contrast to that of Voltairean
man, for whom God's purpose, far from being inscrutable, is
crystal-clear. He has been endowed with an instinctive self-love,
but this instinct of his prompts him to respect it in others. Social
harmony, in this rosily optimistic view of human nature, arises
from doing what comes naturally. There is no clash of particular
and general interests, no tension between self-regard and regard
for other people. The duties enjoined by God upon man are
fulfilled by following our natural inclinations. Alexander Pope
expresses this cosy optimism in his *Essay on Man* (Epistle IV):

Self-love but serves the virtuous mind to wake,
As the small pebble stirs the peaceful lake;
The centre mov'd, a circle strait succeeds,
Another still, and still another spreads;
Friend, parent, neighbour, first it will embrace,
His country next, and next all human race;

Pascal's 'barbarous' 'S'il y a un Dieu, il ne faut aimer que lui, et non les créatures' (RX, p.168) had prompted Voltaire to evoke the same all-embracing love of mankind in much the same terms as Pope: 'Il faut aimer très tendrement les créatures; il faut aimer sa patrie, sa femme, son père, ses enfants; et il faut si bien les aimer que Dieu nous les fait aimer malgré nous'. 'We must love one another and die': Voltaire would have agreed with W.H. Auden. The thought of what lies beyond the grave should not trouble a sensible man; Hamlet's musings and the English propensity to suicide had struck a responsive chord in Voltaire but that did nothing to change his fundamental attitude to life: 'Quel est l'homme sage qui sera prêt à se pendre, parce qu'il ne sait pas comme on voit Dieu face à face' (RVI, pp.165-66), 'adorons Dieu sans vouloir percer dans l'obscurité de ses mystères' (RXII, p. 169). Life is for the living and death a natural phenomenon, the prospect of which should not impair the bracing realisation that 'de tous les animaux, l'homme est le plus parfait, le plus heureux et celui qui vit le plus longtemps' (RXXVIII, p.175).

The cosmic optimism of the final *lettre philosophique* complements Voltaire's sanguine account of the stable, well-regulated microcosm of Georgian England. His scrutiny of human nature convinced him that the role which had been assigned to man in God's creation was not a spectacular one and required neither great feats of moral heroism nor even much altruism. Mandeville's formula, 'private vices, public benefits', sums up not only the individual's contribution to the dynamic of capitalism but also his conformity with the Divine plan as Voltaire saw it. Enlightened self-interest was the foundation of the commercial success and the general prosperity and happiness of the English nation as a whole. Pascal's dramatic presentation of 'la misère de l'homme' (RVI, p.165) is countered by a response in a deliberately lower key from Voltaire. This takes the form of an extract from a letter from his friend Everard Fawkener, healthy, wealthy and wise in his unalloyed contentment with a life of virtuous bourgeois mediocrity. It seems entirely fitting that having banished heroes of the traditional sort — the 'illustres méchants' (XII, p.76) — from his account of England, Voltaire should have chosen to conduct the defence of humanity against the misanthropic Pascal by setting against him that archetypal anti-hero and benefactor of mankind, the English merchant.

4 *Structure and Style*

Voltaire's decision to add the 'anti-Pascal' to the French version of his letters on the English was strengthened by his belief that it would not impair the coherence of the work. 'Cela fera un livre d'une grosseur raisonnable sans qu'il y ait rien de hors d'œuvre', he wrote to Thieriot (D631). His concern for cohesion is equally evident in the preceding letters, where the thread of continuity is maintained fairly unobtrusively by thematic links or by the repetition at the beginning of a letter of a word or phrase used at the end of the previous one. The word which is picked up in this way is often a key word in the conceptual framework of the work as a whole and the echo is quite clear. The final sentence of the ninth letter, for example, is in close correlation with the opening sentence of the following letter. The vocabulary ('paysans [...] qui ne dédaignent pas de continuer à cultiver la terre qui les a enrichis et dans laquelle ils vivent libres') is repeated: 'Le commerce, qui a enrichi les citoyens en Angleterre a contribué à les rendre libres'. The liberty and prosperity of contemporary England is the theme; the transition from the agricultural to the commercial context provides the variation.

The chain joining politics in Letters VIII and IX to commerce in Letter X is extended by another link to include the eleventh letter on inoculation. The link is less obvious but equally effective; the geographical connection between 'Surate' and 'Caire' mentioned in the last sentence of Letter X and Circassia referred to several times in the following letter probably occurs to the reader only at the subliminal level. The relation between the commercial interests of the Circassians and the practice of inoculation is soon brought home to him however in unequivocal terms: 'Une nation commerçante est toujours fort alerte sur ses intérêts et ne néglige rien des connaissances qui peuvent être utiles à son négoce'. The eminently useful merchant described in the final sentence of Letter X is clearly evoked by this statement, and his contribution to the sum of human happiness through the enhancement of the quality of life is the theme which is carried through the rest of the letter on inoculation and used as a link to introduce, in the preamble to the following letter, the next group (Letters XII-XVII) in which human achievement is judged in terms of the benefits accruing to mankind.

Letters XXIII and XXIV may be seen to fit into this scheme quite well. The twentieth letter ('Sur les seigneurs qui cultivent les lettres') links up with the earlier ones insofar as it is a vindication of the ideal of a cultured élite, exercising a salutary influence on the community to which its members belong: 'leur état est d'avoir l'esprit cultivé, comme celui d'un marchand est de connaître son négoce' (pp.132-33). Official encouragement of science and the arts and recognition of their essentially high status in any well regulated society are understandably advocated by Voltaire in Letter XXIII. But public patronage is seen by him in the following letter as having a duty to the educated public at large, a responsibility to see that theory is wedded to practice, and research and scholarship applied to some desirable social purpose. The utilitarian approach dominates Voltaire's thinking on this subject, as on all others discussed in the *Lettres philosophiques*, and constitutes a powerful unifying influence.

The literary craftsman's preoccupation with welding together disparate elements to form a unified structure, however, is not the fundamental source of the work's unity, which arises rather from Voltaire's emergent philosophy of history. Voltaire's view of Hanoverian England is subordinated to his more general perspective upon the evolution of civilisation, which in turn is governed by the basic relationship between God and man perceived in 'anti-Pascalian' terms. The pervasive spirit of liberty in English life and institutions is the dominant theme of the work, but this spirit is seen to operate within certain limitations of space and time. Man's freedom is curtailed by the necessary conditions of his existence, determined by God's will. Voltaire is keenly aware of the influence upon a particular situation of the external factors of environment and the accumulated weight of events. This 'conjoncture', the inevitable combination of specific circumstances, he sees as crucially important; it tempers his judgement of the impact which any human being, however great, can make upon history. 'Venir au monde à propos' (VII, p.52), a phrase he will use often in his later works, sums up this aspect of his approach. It applies to his treatment of both men of action (Cardinal de Retz, Cromwell) and men of letters (Voiture, Shakespeare). Individuals are not, for all that, reduced to mere cyphers. Throughout the letters, Voltaire, whilst primarily offering evaluations of the creative work of writers and philosophers, is also concerned with the personality of his subjects. He professes to be unconcerned with character: 'je ne considère les gens après leur mort que par leurs ouvrages' (XXI, p.139). This is belied by his treatment of Clarke who is brought to life with a few deft strokes (VII, p.51); by his attempt to rehabilitate Bacon with a magnanimous judgement (XII, p.77); and above all by his generous references to Descartes, 'estimable même dans ses égarements' (XIV, p.94) both intellectual and carnal. Espousing 'le parti de l'humanité', Voltaire succeeds in arousing sympathy for a Descartes with more than a passing resemblance to himself and diametrically opposed to the superhuman Newton, flawless to the point of unreality. The biographical elements in the *Lettres philosophiques* lend colour and body to the text; the verdict which Voltaire renders on Descartes's life (and not just his life's work) sums up the motivating force underlying all the letters: 'il éprouva tout ce qui appartient à l'humanité' (XIV, p.91).

Voltaire is already, in the *Lettres philosophiques*, self-consciously fighting the good fight to protect humane values against the forces of darkness. 'Ecraser l'infâme', the rousing war cry of his crusade against these forces in the later years of his life, will serve to recall his spirited defence of the enlightened thought and behaviour he perceived in so many aspects of contemporary English life. For him, taking up the cudgels implied something more subtle, however, than crushing the enemy by the brute force of invective; the polemical skill which is evident in the literary strategy and tactics deployed in these letters foreshadows his later mastery in this field.

On both the strategic and tactical levels, Voltaire's main weapon is comparison. The reader is constantly called upon to compare and contrast, weigh pros and cons and move towards a judgement which may, but does not always, involve a straight choice between opposites. He is presented in the very first word of the first sentence of the first letter with a narrator who goes on to describe a confrontation between himself and an engaging and entirely prepossessing Quaker. Both these fictional *personae* are deftly etched in. Voltaire distances himself from his narrator, who, besides 'la curiosité d'un homme raisonnable' which he ascribes to himself (and which Voltaire himself would not disown), is endowed with a degree of naivety which his above-average creator clearly associates with the average Frenchman of his day. The presentation of the characters through the eyes of the narrator places upon the reader the onus of interpreting the dialogue between the two. Voltaire deliberately creates this source of ambiguity, it would seem, so as to preclude a straightforwardly partisan reaction from the reader. Forcing him to take sides would not be consistent with the global strategy of the work, which aims at extolling a fair-minded, well-balanced appreciation of contrary views and the peaceful co-existence of opposites. The reader, from the beginning, is being induced to stand back, award points and judge between the contesting parties. The idea that no single individual or group has a monopoly of truth and that tolerance of diverse beliefs is a positive good is already being adumbrated.

The first letter is, in this sense, a fitting prelude to all those which follow. The brilliance of the technique employed in it, however, quickly fades. Quaker doctrine purveyed in the second letter, as in the first, through the lively conversation of our avid Frenchman and his English informant gives way to Quaker history, and the crisply functional voice of Voltaire (later to become familiar to readers of his *contes*) takes over to the detriment of the embryonic character of the narrator who soon sinks to the level of a colourless 'je' addressing a fictional and even more colourless 'vous' across the Channel. Although the absence of the element of physical confrontation detracts from the interest of the other letters on religion, the comparative aspect continues to be used to good effect. Binary oppositions (like that between the ebullient French *abbé* and the relatively inert English clergyman in Letter V) are extended to give a triple focus (the 'jeune et vif bachelier français', 'théologien anglican' and 'presbytérien d'Ecosse' of Letter VI). These animated vignettes are followed by the evocation of the bustling activity of a Stock Exchange whose community of purpose is vividly underlined by the stringing together of diverse religious groups — 'le juif, le mahométan et le chrétien'; 'le presbytérien [...] l'anabaptiste [...] l'anglican [...] le quaker'. The harmonious pluralism which is thus vindicated in the religious life of England has its counterpart in the area of English politics and Voltaire's propagandist aims are achieved by similar means. In Letter VIII ('Sur le parlement') he takes up a comparative standpoint and introduces a third point of reference: Rome. Explicit comparisons between Rome and England are used first of all to suggest implicit comparisons between England and France before Voltaire contrasts the latter pair directly to England's advantage. 'Pesez [...], et jugez' is the final directive to the reader, who probably feels that the scales of judgement have been heavily weighted in the foregoing letter. The idea of balance, however, remains central to its picture of the constitutional machinery of England; and this idea of a just distribution of political power will be coupled in the following two letters with that of the emergence of a substantial measure of social justice and harmony, as English history is taken to illustrate the gradual elimination of the more glaring inequalities.

Throughout the letters on English literature and thought, the comparative approach continues to provide the basic instrument of analysis in the familiar form of contrasting features of French and English civilisation — the Académie Française and the Royal Society, Rabelais and Swift, Descartes and Newton. The tendency already noted in the earlier letters to widen the comparison into a three-fold one is equally evident and may be correlated with Voltaire's growing attachment to the ternary patterns which will characterise the syntax and style of his more mature prose works. In a more general way, this tendency points

towards the broader synthesis of values which is meant to
emerge from a balanced judgement of the detailed analyses of
the text of the *Lettres philosophiques*. The final paragraphs of
Letter XXII make this clear: after dismissing English
historiography, vitiated by partisan spirit ('la moitié de la nation
est toujours l'ennemie de l'autre'), Voltaire extols the ideal of
literary commerce and exchange which is reflected in the
balance-sheet of the intellectual relations between France,
England and Italy and opens up the grand vista of a sort of
cultural Common Market in which enlightened cosmopolitanism
would prevail.

The same movement characterises the 'anti-Pascal' in which a
positive set of values crystallises around Voltaire's fundamental
opposition to the seventeenth-century philosopher's view of life.
The physical encounter of narrator and Quaker in the first letter
is matched by the strong sense of confrontation in the final one.
Whereas Voltaire was merely the puppet-master in the first
dialogue, he steps into the arena himself to take on the
redoubtable Pascal. Literary art is abandoned for the more
explicit articulation of plain truths about man's real-life
situation, and the subtlety and fruitful ambiguity which
characterised the opening letter are branded in the final one as
essentially Pascalian features of a mystical and mystifying view
of life. Sadly, the reader must attune his ear to the voice of
Voltaire, the commentator, the compulsive writer of marginalia.

Even if one regrets the way Voltaire chose to round off his
Lettres, one cannot deny the force of his straightforward
advocacy of 'la saine philosophie' in his final remarks to his
readers. The richly suggestive first letter had allowed the reader
to act as accountant and to decide what was to be put on the
debit and what on the credit side for the Quakers. The
rationality of their ethical doctrine shines out in their favour and
will be echoed in Voltaire's reduction of Christian teaching to 'la
simplicité, l'humanité, la charité' in his first remark on the fine-
drawn metaphysical distinctions of Pascal. The irrational
elements of their faith however begin to disturb the 'homme
raisonnable' (narrator and reader) from the moment of the visit
to the Quaker meeting-house in Letter II. Thereafter, the

'enthousiasme' which colours the history of this sect is recalled by the anti-humanist stance of the Presbyterians in Letter VI and later again in Letter XXIII by the anathema cast upon social diversions by the rabid Puritan, Prynne. These preliminary skirmishes may be seen as leading up to the all-out assault on Pascal in Letter XXV.

The rational factor can be seen at its demystifying work in the style as well as in the content of the *Lettres philosophiques*. Voltaire's commentary on selected *Pensées* of Pascal continues to use some of the stylistic devices which have already been tellingly employed to serve his propagandist aims in the earlier letters. The stark binary oppositions in Pascal's view of man are countered by Voltaire's attempt to offer a unitary view of a multi-faceted human nature: in his view, 'les différences qui sont en nous sont si peu contradictoires qu'il serait contradictoire qu'elles n'existassent pas' (RIV, p.163). Contrasting features are juxtaposed but in an inclusive rather than a divisive way. The fundamental theme of man as a composite creature, 'mêlé de mal et de bien, de plaisir et de peine' (RIII, p.163) is illustrated by Voltaire's treatment of Pascal in the short introduction to his critical remarks where he is presented as 'ce misanthrope sublime'. The full scale work which might have emerged from the *Pensées* is envisaged as 'un livre plein de paralogismes éloquents et de faussetés admirablement déduites'. The effective use of qualifying adjective or modifying adverb with the noun immediately establishes Voltaire's stance vis-à-vis the uncompromisingly antithetical phrases of the first extract from Pascal and the attitude they represent. The oxymorons used in the *Lettres philosophiques* vary in the piquancy of the contrast they introduce, but most of them throw a searching light upon nebulous concepts or dubious practices, e.g. heroism and greatness ('d'illustres méchants', XII, p.76; 'brillante folie de faire des conquêtes', VIII, p.55); religious fervour and misplaced zeal ('saintement fou', III, p.30; 'une grande habitude d'inspiration', III, p.31; la pieuse ambition d'être les maîtres', V, p.42).

Voltaire is determined to strip Pascal's view of man of its mystical trappings and to lay bare the plain truth of human

existence: 'l'homme n'est point une énigme' (RIII, p.162). This
attitude has been made evident from the very first letter, in
which the technique of reducing symbolic or otherwise
significant actions to their meaningless physical rudiments
(which was to become a characteristic feature of Voltaire's
approach to satire) is applied to baptism ('jeter de l'eau froide
sur la tête, avec un peu de sel', p.21) and to the would-be
impressive accessories of an army recruiting campaign ('des
meurtriers vêtus de rouge, avec un bonnet haut de deux pieds,
enrôlent des citoyens en faisant du bruit avec deux petits bâtons
sur une peau d'âne bien tendu', p.24). The same reductive zest
characterises the operation of cutting down to size fellow human
beings who forget that compared with 'le Très-Haut' they are
only 'des vers de terre' (p.23) — a point which is underlined in
the final letter's comment on human presumption: 'ce n'est
point à nous d'oser interroger la Providence' (RXIII, pp.169-
70).

The sustained eloquence of Pascal is admired and respected by
his adversary but hardly matched in the *Lettres philosophiques*.
Voltaire in his narrative or expository vein is briskly (and
admirably) purposeful and keeps his promise to write 'sans
verbiage' (XV, p.96). He does not allow such disciplined
economy to stifle his natural vivacity however, and his persistent
rhetorical soliciting of the reader's favour enlivens the letters. In
the thirteenth letter 'Sur M. Locke' for example, he manipulates
his audience by using a number of different voices to articulate
arguments and counter-arguments which are all calculated to
win approval of 'la sage et modeste philosophie de Locke'
(p.87). This may be seen if one compares the temperate tone of
the quoted words of the English philosopher himself 'qu'il ose
avancer modestement' and the equally modest self-introduction
of the narrator ('Si j'osais parler après M. Locke', p.85) with the
ill-mannered dogmatism of the scholastic philosophers ('Ici,
tous les philosophes de l'école m'arrêtent en argumentant, et
disent [...]', p.86), followed by the tersely barbaric contribution
of *le superstitieux*: 'il faut brûler, pour le bien de leurs âmes,
ceux qui soupçonnent qu'on peut penser avec la seule aide du
corps'. The narrator clearly makes way for Voltaire to round off

the 'debate' with a stirring deistic profession of faith in God's omnipotence, and His capacity therefore to endow matter with thought and feeling. Without resorting to such an ambitious orchestration of different voices, Voltaire, in Letter XV, imparts a great deal of animation to his account of Newton's theory of gravity by putting into direct speech the objection against the term 'attraction' voiced by 'presque tous les Français savants et autres' and then allowing Newton to have his say and dispose authoritatively of the 'impulsionnaires'.

Despite the undoubtedly welcome critical attention which has recently been paid to the 'ventriloquism' of Voltaire in the *Lettres philosophiques* (*14*), it is arguable that Voltaire's own, already clearly recognisable voice makes just as powerful an impact upon the reader. Dryly sardonic touches of mock-piety like the playful pirouette executed at the end of Letter V and again in the final sentence of Letter XX; neat encapsulations of good sense tending towards aphorism, like 'il n'y a rien à gagner avec un enthousiaste' (I, p.22) or 'tout commentateur de bons mots est un sot' (XXII, p.142); finely judged variations of sentence length, with short sentences used to effect a striking opening (Letter V) or conclusion (Letter VII): all these anticipate the technique of the mature satiric *prosateur* and *conteur*. In addition the author of the *Lettres philosophiques* must be given credit for the real eloquence which reveals an 'âme sensible' inspired by compassion and the spirit of decency. The fourth paragraph of Letter IX reflects Voltaire's passionate concern for human dignity in long rolling periods which suggest the sense of his affirmation 'Il a fallu des siècles pour rendre justice à l'humanité'. The sense of outrage is even more acute in the final paragraph of Letter XXIII where he inveighs against 'cette barbarie gothique qu'on nomme sévérité chrétienne' in two long sentences in which the torrent of subordinate clauses, checked (as in the previous example) only by a momentary 'dis-je' as he draws breath, is powered by the seething indignation which he still feels for his country's unjust and inhuman refusal to allow the civilised burial of Mlle Lecouvreur, who had added such lustre to its cultural life.

5 Conclusion: 'Ce manifeste des lumières'

'Ce manifeste des lumières': René Pomeau's description of the *Lettres philosophiques* suggests both the special status of this work in the context of the French Enlightenment and the way in which it prefigures Voltaire's well-earned reputation as a militant *philosophe*. It heralded a host of other *œuvres de combat* from him which can be related to it and which demonstrate the essential continuity of his thought.

There can be no mistaking Voltaire's intention of launching an offensive against Roman Catholicism in the *Lettres*. He was only half serious when he suggested to his friend Cideville that his choice of the Jansenists (with Pascal as their most powerful representative) as his main target would win him the favour of their Jesuit opponents (D.630). He would not have been surprised at the hostile reaction of the Jesuits' journal, the *Mémoires de Trévoux* (Jan. 1735, p.96), which deplored his attack upon 'la religion, les moeurs, le gouvernement et tous les bons principes'. His deep-rooted detestation of organised religion and especially of the Catholic Church is evident throughout the work, but it is counter-balanced by a general attachment to 'natural religion' and those elements of it which he detects in the moral doctrines of Socinians, Arians and Quakers. The same abhorrence of superstition, fanaticism and sectarian strife will lead him around 1750 to formulate in the *Sermon des Cinquante* the idea of preserving the healthy, 'natural' core of deism in Christianity whilst excising what, in his view, had been contaminated by Catholicism. Voltaire's hope that such drastic surgery would produce the sort of moderate, ecumenical outlook that characterised the Anglicanism of Hanoverian Britain can be seen in his *Histoire de Jenni* (1775) in the person of the exemplary English clergyman, Dr Freind. If Freind's success in persuading the atheist Burton to leave the ranks of the ungodly and adopt his own deist credo might have tended to surround Voltaire with a faint odour of sanctity, this impression was effectively dispelled on the eve of his death in 1778 by his last published work: the 94 fresh Remarks with which he prefaced a new edition of the *Pensées* by his friend Condorcet, fiercer and more sarcastic in tone than the original 'anti-Pascal'.

The optimistic view of human nature and the future of mankind which colours the 'anti-Pascal' and the preceding account of English society continues to be affirmed in the works which Voltaire produced in the idyllic phase of the period of his relationship with Mme du Châtelet in her château at Cirey in Champagne. The buoyant confidence in scientific progress proclaimed in the letters on Newton provides the impetus for further popularisation of his ideas in the *Eléments de la philosophie de Newton* (1738). The *Eléments* had been preceded by *Le Mondain* (1736) and the *Défense du Mondain* (1737): a renewed profession of faith in the mercantilism of the *Lettres philosophiques* now based on the economic doctrine of luxury as a utilitarian objective in the pursuit of happiness. The high point of the Cirey period is marked by the cosmic optimism of the *Traité de métaphysique* (1738), which posits a natural and salutary sociability in human nature in opposition to Pascal's bleak view of the world as 'un assemblage de méchants et de malheureux' (Introduction). The same rejection of Pascal is implicit in the comparison between the exhilarating prospect of the Newtonian universe held out by Voltaire in *Micromégas* (the first version of which is generally taken to date from 1739) and the anguish of Pascal before the vastness of interstellar space.

Optimism as a philosophical doctrine was presented in the eighteenth century in perhaps its most popular and accessible form by Pope in the four epistles of his *Essay on Man* (1733-34). The context of this work owed a great deal to the intellectual converse between Pope and his mentor in philosophy, Bolingbroke. Voltaire's reaction to the *Essay* was conveyed to Cideville: he saw the poem as 'la paraphrase de mes petites remarques sur Pascal' (D915, 20 Sept. 1735). The final sentence of the sixth *Remarque* of Letter XXV certainly echoes Pope's 'Whatever is, is right' even more clearly than Voltaire's own summing-up for Cideville: 'Il [Pope] prouve en beaux vers que la nature de l'homme a toujours été et toujours dû être ce qu'elle est'. Voltaire's enthusiastic reading of Pope's poem led him to model upon it his own *Discours sur l'Homme*, the first six of which appeared in 1739 and the final one in 1742.

However resolved Voltaire was to look on the bright side of life, his psychological make-up ensured that cheerful resignation to divine Providence could not be sustained indefinitely. The optimistic belief in man's ability to shape his life through adopting an activist approach is the dominant strain in the *Lettres philosophiques*, but there is also a counter-balancing tendency to stress man's limitations. The constraints placed upon man's freedom of action by his environment and the age in which he lives will be a recurring theme in Voltaire's work from the *Lettres philosophiques* onwards. The interplay of human agency and historical determinism which will constitute a significant element of Voltaire's philosophy of history in his major historical writings can already be seen in the *Lettres*.

Philosophical optimism takes a battering in *Candide* (1759) mainly because of Voltaire's antipathy to its passive acquiescence in the face of rampant evil. The world of *Candide* is Pascal's 'assemblage de méchants et de malheureux' and it is the one that Voltaire has come to recognise as a reality. In this world free will is illusory: Man proposes, God disposes. Voltaire's determinism, submerged in the *Lettres philosophiques* by his insistence on the freedom pervading all aspects of English life and institutions, came to the fore after 1748 and remained as a constant element in his thought to the end of his life. 'Machines de la Providence' (*L'Ingénu*, 1768) men may be, but they are machines designed to work on their own within prescribed limits. Candide and his companions accept this in-built compulsion to act purposefully as a basis for a moderate degree of contentment. This muted optimism is a very faint echo of the resounding call to action of the 'anti-Pascal' (RXXIII) but it is nonetheless resilient and will remain an integral part of Voltaire's philosophical outlook. The *Lettres philosophiques* certainly reflect the heady optimism of Voltaire's Cirey period, but they also foreshadow in their presentation of historical necessity the more sober resignation of the disabused *philosophe*, whose efforts to change the world will be tempered by his realisation that 'la terre, les hommes et les animaux sont ce qu'ils doivent être dans l'ordre de la Providence' (RVI, p.166).

The strain of determinism which characterises all Voltaire's work in the last thirty years of his life never succeeds in vanquishing his attachment to the ideal of vigorous action. In this connection, the England he had chosen as his second country remained for him a shining light, an idealised model of what an enterprising free society could offer its members. His enthusiasm for the political regime of a limited monarchy based on the checks and balances of a constitution in which all sections of society were supposedly represented never waned. The succinct exposition of English parliamentary democracy in the eighth *lettre philosophique* is elaborated but never basically altered in Voltaire's later works, as may be seen from his description in Chapter VIII of *La Princesse de Babylone* (1768):

> ...le plus parfait gouvernement peut-être qui soit aujourd'hui dans le monde. Un roi honoré et riche, tout-puissant pour faire le bien, impuissant pour faire le mal, est à la tête d'une nation libre, guerrière, commerçante et éclairée. Les grands d'un côté et les représentants des villes de l'autre, partagent la législation avec le monarque.

The accent which Voltaire puts upon constitutional restraints serves to remind us of his unswerving allegiance throughout his life to the literary discipline imposed by neoclassicism. He reacted strongly against the wave of anglomania in the 1760s and was particularly incensed by the later attempts of such champions of Shakespeare as La Place and Letourneur to introduce Bardolatry into France. He continued however to guard jealously his own claim to primacy in introducing Shakespeare to his compatriots and in his undeniable role as a populariser it may be noted that the method employed in the *Lettres philosophiques* of sifting the wheat (as he saw it) from the chaff is no different from his latter-day culling of gems from the vast Shakespearian œuvre: 'perles dans son énorme fumier'. His career as a dramatist, from *Œdipe* (1718) to *Irène* (1778), spans the whole of his creative life and it illustrates the permanence of his jackdaw-like instinct for seizing upon and assimilating elements in the drama of other countries which could serve to vivify without impairing French neoclassicism. A prudent literary cosmopolitanism of this sort was part of the legacy of his early contact with English life. Nature had been saluted in 1734, 'l'arbre touffu' had been admired, but 'l'arbre [taillé] des jardins de Marly' (XVIII, p.124) always represented for Voltaire the superior claims of culture. As the Patriarch pungently put it to an English visitor somewhat over-enthusiastic in his advocacy of Shakespeare's unbridled genius: 'Avec permission, Monsieur, mon cul est bien dans la nature et cependant je porte des culottes'.

This civilised sentiment was perhaps so earthily expressed in order to show Voltaire's admiration for English forthrightness. He certainly continued throughout the whole of his life to regard England as, on the whole, an enlightened country whose citizens 'ont quelque chose de plus ferme, de plus réfléchi, de plus opiniâtre que quelques autres peuples' (*Dictionnaire philosophique*. Art, Gouvernement, 1771). This vision of an ideal community, at the centre of his aspirations as an enlightened patriot, provided the main inspiration for the *Lettres philosophiques*. Over a quarter of a century after their publication, their author's ardent Anglophilia is still being eagerly, if playfully, paraded before English visitors by their would-be fellow-citizen: 'The English [...] are I swear by God Himself, the first Nation in Europe, and if ever I smell of a Resurrection, or come a second time on earth, I will pray God to make me born in England, the Land of Liberty'.

Select Bibliography

EDITIONS

1. *Lettres philosophiques*, édition critique avec une introduction et un commentaire par Gustave Lanson. Nouveau tirage revu et complété par André-M. Rousseau (Paris, Librairie Marcel Didier, 1964) 2 vols. This edition is an essential aid to any detailed study of the work.
2. *Lettres philosophiques ou Lettres anglaises avec le texte complet des remarques sur les Pensées de Pascal*, introduction, notes, choix de variantes, et rapprochements par Raymond Naves (Paris, Classiques Garnier, 1964). The *rapprochements* are particularly useful for situating this text in the more detailed context of Voltaire's total *œuvre*.
3. *Lettres philosophiques*, ed. F.A. Taylor (Oxford, Basil Blackwell, 1943). An excellent edition with good notes, both informative and critical.
4. *Lettres sur les Anglais*, ed. A. Wilson-Green (Cambridge, Cambridge University Press, 1946). Obviously outdated by more recent scholarship, this school edition is still serviceable.
5. *Voltaire: Letters on England*, translated with an introduction by L. Tancock (Penguin Classics, 1980). Certain difficulties of interpretation may be resolved for some readers by consulting this work.

CRITICISM

(SVEC = Studies on Voltaire and the Eighteenth Century)

6. T.J. Barling, 'The literary art of the *Lettres philosophiques*', *SVEC*, XLI (1966), pp.7-69.
7. T. Besterman, ed., *Voltaire on Shakespeare*, *SVEC*, LIV (1967).
8. G. Bonno, *La Culture et la civilisation britanniques devant l'opinion française (1713-1734)* (Philadelphia, American Philosophical Society, 1948).
9. Harcourt Brown, 'The composition of the *Letters Concerning the English Nation*', in W.H. Barber *et al.*, edd., *The Age of the Enlightenment: Studies Presented to Theodore Besterman* (Edinburgh, Oliver and Boyd, 1967), pp.15-34.
10. J.R. Carré, *Reflexions sur l'anti-Pascal de Voltaire* (Paris, Alcan, 1935).
11. P.M. Conlon, *Voltaire's Literary Career from 1728 to 1750*, *SVEC*, XIV (1961).
12. Gavin de Beer and André-Michel Rousseau, *Voltaire's British Visitors*, *SVEC*, XLIX (1967).

13. Roland Desné, 'The role of England in Voltaire's polemic against Pascal: a propos the twenty-fifth *Philosophical Letter*', in *Eighteenth-Century Studies Presented to Arthur M. Wilson* (New York, Russell & Russell, 1972), pp.40-57.

14. Julia L. Epstein, 'Voltaire's ventriloquism: voices in the first *Lettre philosophique*', *SVEC*, CLXXXII (1979), pp.219-35.

15. Peter Gay, *Voltaire's Politics: the Poet as Realist*, 2nd ed., (New Jersey, Princeton University Press, 1965) (Ch. I, 'England: a nation of philosophers', pp.33-65).

16. Ahmad Gunny, *Voltaire and English Literature*, *SVEC*, CLXXVII (1979).

17. A. Lantoine, *Les Lettres philosophiques de Voltaire* (Paris, Malfère, 1931).

18. Haydn Mason, *Voltaire* (London, Hutchinson, 1975). Ch. 5, pp.109-124.

19. Norma Perry, 'Voltaire's view of England', *Journal of European Studies*, VII (1977), pp.77-94.

20. —— 'French and English merchants in the eighteenth century; Voltaire revisited', in *Studies in Eighteenth-Century French Literature Presented to Professor Robert Niklaus* (University of Exeter, 1975), pp.192-213.

21. —— *Sir Everard Fawkener, Friend and Correspondent of Voltaire*, *SVEC*, CXXXIII (1975).

22. R. Pomeau, *La Religion de Voltaire* (Paris, Nizet, 1956).

23. —— *Politique de Voltaire* (Paris, Armand Colin, 1963).

24. —— 'Les *Lettres philosophiques*: le projet de Voltaire' in *Voltaire and the English, Transactions of the Oxford Colloquium (May 1978)*, *SVEC*, CLXXIX (1979), pp.11-24.

25. Marsha Reisler, 'Rhetoric and dialectic in Voltaire's *Lettres philosophiques*', *L'Esprit Créateur*, XVII (Winter 1977), 4, pp.311-24.

26. A.-M. Rousseau, *L'Angleterre et Voltaire*, *SVEC*, CXLV-CXLVII (1976).

27. —— 'Naissance d'un livre et d'un texte: les *Letters concerning the English nation*', in *Voltaire and the English*, *SVEC*, CLXXIX (1979), pp.25-46.

28. Ira O. Wade, *The Intellectual Development of Voltaire* (New Jersey, Princeton University Press, 1969).

29. F.D. White, *Voltaire's Essay on Epic Poetry* (Albany, Brandow, 1915).

GEORGIAN ENGLAND

30. D. Marshall, *Eighteenth-Century England* (London, Longman, 1962).

31. J.H. Plumb, *England in the Eighteenth Century,* The Pelican History of England, 7 (Harmondsworth, Penguin Books, 1950).

32. Roy Porter, *English Society in the Eighteenth Century*, The Pelican Social History of Britain (Harmondsworth, Penguin Books, 1982).

33. W.A. Speck, *Stability and Strife, England 1714-1760*, New History of England, 6 (London, Arnold, 1977).

CRITICAL GUIDES TO FRENCH TEXTS

edited by
Roger Little, Wolfgang van Emden, David Williams